Water Bombers

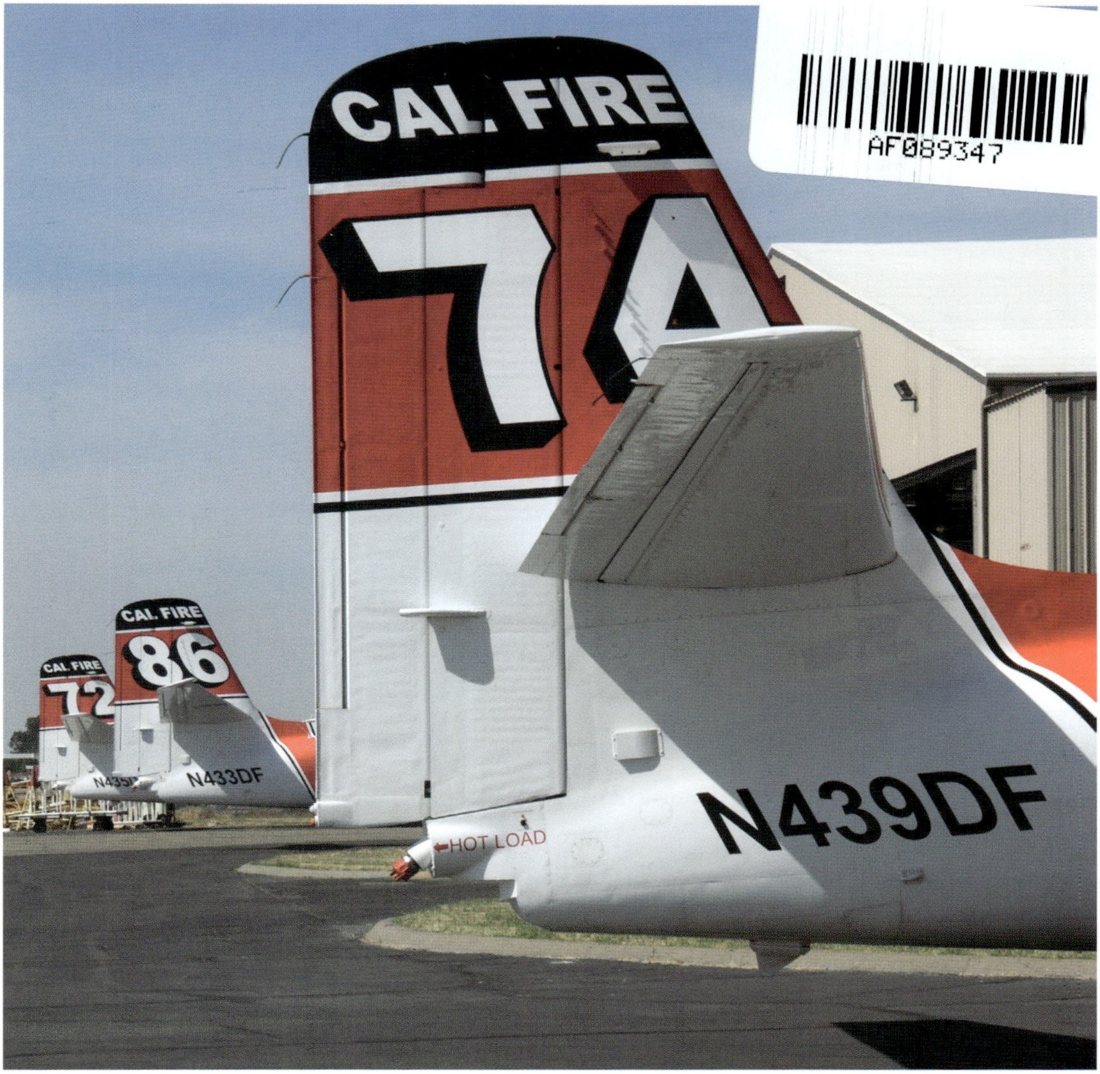

GERRY MANNING

KEY Books

Back cover image: Pictured dropping water at Luqa, Malta, in 2004 is Canadair CL-415 of the Italian Protezione Civile.

Title page image: A line-up of three Cal Fire Grumman S-2T Turbo Tracker water bombers are pictured at McClelland in May 2019.

Contents page image: A pair of Aero Union's Aerostar conversions of the Lockheed P-3 Orion are pictured on the ramp at the company base of Chico, California, in October 2001.

Acknowledgements

Thanks are due to Bob O'Brien for the rescanning of a number of slides and to Ian Atkinson and Steve Williams for some of the pictures. Photographs without a credit are my own.

Published by Key Books
An imprint of Key Publishing Ltd
PO Box 100
Stamford
Lincs PE19 1XQ

www.keypublishing.com

The right of Gerry Manning to be identified as the author of this book has been asserted in accordance with the Copyright, Designs and Patents Act 1988 Sections 77 and 78.

Copyright © Gerry Manning, 2021

ISBN 978 1 80282 146 8

All rights reserved. Reproduction in whole or in part in any form whatsoever or by any means is strictly prohibited without the prior permission of the Publisher.

Typeset by SJmagic DESIGN SERVICES, India.

Contents

Introduction 4
Chapter 1   Forest Fires 5
Chapter 2   Firefighting Aircraft 7
Chapter 3   The Warbirds 8
Chapter 4   Post-War Pistons 33
Chapter 5   Turboprops 72
Chapter 6   Jets 87
Chapter 7   Purpose-Built Water Bombers 97
Chapter 8   Single-Engine Types 107
Chapter 9   Helicopters 111
Chapter 10 The Support Aircraft 122

Introduction

I have been planning this book in my mind for many years, ever since I first became interested in water bombers during my first visit to America in 1979. On that trip, I saw B-17s, Tigercats, Avengers, Privateers, DC-4s, DC-6s and C-119s, all still operational at their bases. Over the years and subsequent tours, I have followed this fascinating and dangerous industry. When I looked up the fates of many of the aircraft I had photographed, it was harrowing to realise how many had been lost in fatal accidents.

This work cannot be a full history of types and operators, as such a book would run into many hundreds of pages. However, it does show the transition from the warbird era to the first of the jets via the intervening years.

Please note, that, owing to the bulk of water bomber activity being in the US, all references to tank volumes refer to the US, not the imperial, gallon.

Gerry Manning, 2021

The Cal Fire base at Porterville has this attractive sign featuring both current and recently operated water bomber types.

Chapter 1
Forest Fires

A forest fire is a naturally occurring event; usually, it is caused by a lightning strike. However, mankind has often been the cause, discarding shards of broken glass bottles that can act as a magnifier of the rays of the sun, and thus causing a hotspot on leaves or twigs that are tinder dry. Also, a poorly supervised campfire can quickly get out of control and spread with alarming speed. A fire in a forest can engulf an area running into tens of thousands of acres of land. Furthermore, being in a forest, they are often many miles from roads or tracks, and a conventionally wheeled fire engine cannot drive to the seat of the blaze and begin to put it out.

The type of forest is also an important factor. For example, a forest could be made up largely of conifer trees; this variety has high resin content and can burn very easily. In full flow, the smoke from a forest fire can rise as high as 20,000ft. This smokestack will have a strong drawing power, and even large aircraft can be sucked into this, with the turbulence making it difficult to control, and, since the drops are at low altitude, it is not unknown for a pilot to lose control and crash.

Not all forest fires occur on flat plains, they can be on the side of a hill or mountain, or, to make the pilot's job even more difficult, in a canyon. In the case of the latter, the aircraft has to fly down the canyon to drop its load of water or retardant upon the fire or its path and then climb away. Taking into account the smoke, lack of visibility and the disturbed air currents, this can all spell danger for the unwary crew. It is of note that, amongst the pictures used to illustrate this work, too high a proportion of these aircraft have come to grief whilst undertaking this most dangerous of flight operations.

To help the aircraft drop their load in the right place, a spotter aircraft will often be circling above the forest to give the water bomber the right path to fly, or to lead the air attack aircraft on the right heading for the drop. In a major blaze with many aircraft dropping, the spotter acts as a 'master bomber', with a fire chief on board to guide each aircraft in and to decide where the loads should be dropped to put out the blaze. The chief also acts as an air traffic controller, so that when several aircraft are dealing with the fire, they are kept safely apart.

For simplicity for the reader, the phrase 'water bomber' has and will be used throughout this book. However, in most cases of land-based aircraft, it is not water that is dropped but a chemical retardant that is laid down in a line of the fire's approach, with the aim of halting its progress. The first chemical used was sodium calcium borate, developed in the US in 1954 by the US Borax Company. The chemical was mixed with water, and this resulted in a heavy white sticky liquid substance that was fire-resistant for some hours after being dropped. The great problem with this was it was quite toxic, and when large quantities were used it could sterilise the soil. A replacement came in 1959, with a new compound called Bentonite; added to this was a pinkish dye, enabling the drop pilot and spotter aircraft to see exactly where the drop had been placed. This compound has also been superseded by several new brands. One is Phos-Chek, which consists of 80 per cent water, 14 per cent fertilising salts and 6 per cent colouring agent, corrosion inhibitors and flow conditioners. The second brand in use is Fire-Trol LCR-R. This is basically liquid ammonium polyphosphate with concentrated attapulgite clay to suspend the colour and add visibility. It contains a corrosion inhibitor and iron oxide for colour, and is simply mixed with the required amount of water. One ton of liquid will produce 923 gallons of retardant to be directly pumped into the tanks of the aircraft. Both retardant types will also help to regenerate new growth, thanks to the fertiliser element of the compound.

Despite the forests being painted red by the retardant, the colour is designed to fade to a natural earth tan after a few days of direct sunshine. When flying over the tanker bases, it is easy to spot their ramps as the concrete is often stained pink and stands out. Even though it has not been used for many years, borate has given its name to the process and some people still refer to the aircraft as 'borate bombers'.

Water is the main weapon of the sea or lake skimming amphibians to combat fires. The aircraft will lower scoops either side of the fuselage and skim across a body of water to fill their internal tanks. They will then return to the fire and drop the water onto the blaze, either in one dump or several, depending upon the needs of the fire chief in control.

In May 2009, a trio of North American OV-10 Broncos at McClellan await the flights to their summer bases.

Chapter 2
Firefighting Aircraft

What are the aircraft types used as water bombers? The simple answer is almost any surplus aeroplane can be used. For many years, they were always propeller-driven warplanes or cargo carriers, but, in recent years, older jet airliners that have been superseded by more fuel-efficient models have begun to be seen on the ramps of the air attack bases (the phrase used by the state of California for their operations). It had been usual to convert older low-value airframes for this limited and specialised task; dependent on how wet or dry a season is, the water bomber may not fly a great deal. Engines are run on a regular basis, and every two weeks an aircraft is test flown for the crew to practise their skills, during which they will perform a water drop on a local airfield. Newly built aircraft are expensive to buy, and few private operators can afford to have them sit around in a wet summer with little utilisation.

An example of a contractor, a Coulson C-130, and a Cal Fire S-2T Tracker sharing the ramp at Porterville in May 2019.

Chapter 3
The Warbirds

The smallest air tanker to be used was the Boeing PT-17 Stearman. The type first flew in 1934 and was a biplane trainer used in World War Two in great numbers, with more than 8,000 airframes being produced before production was terminated. The powerplant for the aircraft was a single 220hp Continental R-670-5 air cooled radial piston engine. The summer of 1956 saw the California Division of Forestry (CDF), now known as the California Department of Forestry and Fire Protection, (Cal Fire), use the Stearman loaded with either 100 gallons of borate or 125 gallons of water. This was not deemed sufficient, so, in 1957, the federal US Forestry Service (USFS) started to operate the Grumman TBM Avenger, fitted with a 625-gallon tank. It had first been operated by private contractors, which had converted the type in 1954. The Avenger was a World War Two naval torpedo bomber, which first flew in August 1941 and entered service with the US Navy (USN) in time for the June 1942 Battle of Midway. It remained in service in a number of different roles with the fleet until 1954. The aircraft was powered by a single 1,900hp Wright R2600-20 radial piston and it could still be found in service as a water bomber into the mid-1990s on the eastern seaboard of Canada, in the province of New Brunswick.

During the 1980s, as the authorities moved away from single-engine water bombers for reasons of safety, many Avengers were acquired by collectors for use as warbirds. They had their tanks removed, and the airframe returned to its wartime configuration and was painted in a period colour scheme. They can be found at airshows and are still flown by enthusiasts for their pleasure.

Another former USN type operated as a water bomber was the Grumman AF-2 Guardian. Its role was to be a carrier-borne, anti-submarine search and strike aircraft. The powerplant was a single 2,400hp Pratt & Whitney R-2800-48 radial piston engine. It first flew in December 1946 and served with the USN until the middle of 1957, when the last reserve unit in New York retired the type. Only a handful of Guardians were converted, each equipped with an 850-gallon tank during the late 1950s and flown by Aero Union from their base at Chico, California, until the early 1970s. A decade later, the remains of the fleet, both converted and unconverted, were still to be found at Chico. They have since been acquired by collectors to fly, or by museums.

One of the most stylish water bombers was also one of the fastest. It was the twin-engine, single-seat, carrier-borne fighter, the Grumman F7F Tigercat. The engines were a pair of 2,100hp P&W R-2800 radial pistons. November 1943 saw the first flight, and it was operated until the late 1940s. The type was an early conversion, being used in the 1948 summer season in the state of Oregon. The retardant was initially carried in modified drop tanks under each wing. However, this was not a particularly successful method, as the pattern of ground coverage was not very effective. Eventually an 800-gallon tank was fitted under the centre of the fuselage, later upped to a 1,000-gallon one. One of the great advantages of the type's speed was it could get to a fire quickly and nip it in the bud before it grew too large, without the need to fly repeated sorties to follow up. The type was in service with two California-based companies, TMB Inc and Sis-Q Flying Service (later known as Macavia), until the early 1980s, when the aircraft were snapped up by the warbird movement. They can be seen flying to this day at airshows and have even been raced at the Reno Air Races in Nevada.

A bomber aircraft is a good candidate for conversion to the peaceful role of fighting forest fires, as it can be adapted to have the retardant/water tank placed in the bomb bay. One such type was the

Douglas A-26 Invader; in uniform, it took part in World War Two, Korea, Vietnam, with the French in Indo-China, the CIA in the *Bay of Pigs* operation in Cuba in 1962 and the civil war in Nigeria over the breakaway province of Biafra in 1967. The 'A' in its designation stood for 'attack' when originally in service with the US Army Air Force, it first flying in July 1942. When the newly independent US Air Force (USAF) was formed post-war, they abandoned the 'A for attack' designation in June 1948 and changed it to 'B for bomber'. During World War Two, the designation B-26 was carried by the Martin Marauder, but it was no longer in service by 1948. Some operators have called the Invader the A-26, others B-26. The type had a long service life as a fire fighter, serving into the new millennium with Air Spray (1967) of Red Deer, Alberta, which operated 18 airframes. Other users have included Conair of Abbotsford, British Colombia, which flew eight into the late 1980s, and Lynch Flying Tankers of Billings, Montana. This company provided pilots and aircraft for the A-26s in the 1989 film *Always*, directed by Steven Spielberg. The film is about water bombers and their pilots and also features a Fairchild C-119 Boxcar and a Consolidated PBY Catalina. It was filmed on locations in Montana and Washington State; real water bomber country.

When Air Spray operated the A-26, they would be contracted by the Alberta Forest Protection Division to provide a fixed number of aircraft at set locations, for a time period of up to 100 days. If this started in the early part of June, the period would run into September and the beginning of the low-risk period. However, if September was very dry, and the risk of fire remained high, then the contracts would be extended. Ten bases would be operational, from Pincher Creek in the south of the province to High Level in the north. Besides the tanker aircraft and pilots, a spotter aircraft would be attached to the base, as well as a small group of ground engineers to keep the old airframes in peak condition. When operational, there were two states of alert: Red and Yellow. In the former, the crew are ready to fly with the spotter aircraft within five minutes, whilst in the latter state it is 30 minutes to be in action. With such a long service in the military, it is of little wonder that so many airframes were converted. The engines for the Invader were a pair of P&W R-2800 radial pistons with a power output of 2,000hp, and most had a 1,200-gallon tank.

Perhaps the most famous of all the American aircraft of World War Two was the Boeing B-17 Flying Fortress. It remained in US military service in minor roles until as late as 1960. This was also the year that the first conversions were made to fight fires. Within what was once the bomb bay, a tank of either 1,800- or 2,000-gallon capacity could be fitted with five doors. The load could then be dropped in a long sequence to make a line, or all at once to put the maximum amount of retardant onto one area. They operated in this role until the mid-1980s, but that was not the end of their lives, as, like the Avenger and Tigercat, they were wanted by the warbird movement or by museums. The B-17 in the Royal Air Force Museum at Hendon was operated by TBM Inc until 1981, before joining the UK collection two years later. Two other former water bombers found fame in film when they appeared in the 1989 remake of the World War Two epic *Memphis Belle*, crossing the Atlantic Ocean to Duxford airfield in Cambridge to recreate the story of the famous B-17 that carried that name.

A number of former US Navy patrol aircraft were converted to water bombers. One such aircraft was the Lockheed PV-2 Harpoon, a five-crew patrol aircraft developed from the Ventura bomber. It first flew at the end of 1943 and was powered by a pair of P&W R-2800 radial piston engines with an output of 2,000hp. The tank fitted had a capacity of 1,000 gallons. Not all the forest protection is in the sunny and dry western states, and one company, Hirth Air Tankers, operated the Harpoon on contracts for the forestry departments in South Carolina and Pennsylvania until at least the late 1990s, being the last commercial operator of the type. The forests in these states run to more than one million acres and are used for the production of paper. Some of the airframes have gone on to join the warbird scene in period military markings.

Another USN patrol aircraft was the Consolidated PBY Catalina. It was an amphibian with a production run of more than 3,000, making it the largest run of any flying boat. Its ability to operate from both land and water means it can either, from land bases, drop retardant or, where there are a lot of lakes, drop water from its 800- or 1,000-gallon tank. In Canada, the aircraft was built under licence and was known as the Canso and would usually operate in the latter mode. The pilot would lower two scoops from under the fuselage and descend to the surface of the lake; these would channel the water into the aircraft's tanks and, when full, would climb back up and drop the water on the fire. In a 15-second run covering 2,000ft, 800 gallons can be scooped up. The Catalina can be found in very limited service in the more remote parts of the Canadian northwest. Many of the earlier operated ones have joined museum collections or fly as warbirds or even luxury flying yachts.

Another Consolidated design was the PB4Y-2 Privateer. It was derived from the B-24 Liberator, and its role was that of a maritime patrol aircraft. The most noticeable difference between the two types was the tall single fin in place of the twin fins of the B-24. As well as this, the fuselage was longer, and the engine nacelles were different. The powerplants were four P&W R-1830-90 radial pistons with an output of 1,350hp each. These engines did not have turbo superchargers, as a maritime patrol aircraft does not fly high like a bomber but roams the seas at a low altitude. A total of 736 aircraft were constructed. The USN operated the type during the Korean War; their role was to drop flares to illuminate road convoys, so as to aid US Marine Corp fighter-bombers that would attack the enemy supply trucks. More than 150 flares could be carried by the Privateer. It was also used by the French Navy, the Aéronavale, in Indo-China. The last role in US military service was that of a drone with the designation QP-4B; these were painted bright red and were destroyed by air-to-air missiles, with the last one shot down at the start of 1964. They were operated from the US Navy Pacific Missile Test Center at Point Mugu, California. It was in the early 1960s that it took up the role of water bomber. A load of 2,500 gallons could be carried in the bomb bay tank. The largest user of the type was Hawkins and Powers Aviation Inc of Greybull, Wyoming, which over the years operated eight examples. They re-engined their aircraft with Wright R-2600 Twin Cyclones with an output of 1,700hp. This extra power was of use on very hot days and bases at higher altitude where the air was thinner. The Privateer had a long career as a water bomber, operating until 2005 when the company ceased trading.

The last of the warbirds is the most impressive; it is the Martin JRM Mars. It was ordered by the US Navy as far back as 1938 and was first flown in July 1942. Only six aircraft were built, five JRM-1s and one JRM-2 with a higher weight. The JRM-1s were modified to this higher weight and designated JRM-3s. They were used as transport flying boats and powered by four Wright Cyclone R-3350 radial piston engines of 2,500hp each. Following a series of disastrous fires in Canada during 1959, a consortium of logging companies, under the leadership of MacMillan Bloedel Ltd, formed Forest Industries Flying Tankers to purchase and operate the last four Mars aircraft, together with a large quantity of spare parts and engines. These aircraft were flown to Victoria, British Colombia, where Fairey Aviation of Canada converted them to their new role. Tanks holding 7,200 gallons were fitted into the cargo bay, as were retractable scoops to upload water whilst taxiing or skimming. Up to 30 tons of water can be taken on board in as little as 22 seconds. In 1987, a foam tank was added with a capacity of 600 gallons. When mixed with water, this can provide an initial insulating barrier, which will then turn into liquid foam and trees on fire absorb this better than plain water.

The size of the aircraft is impressive, with a 200ft wingspan, a length of 120ft and a height of 48ft. Of the original four, two have been lost; one in a crash in 1961 and the other in a hurricane whilst parked in 1962. Each of the Mars had a name of one of the Pacific Islands; the two survivors are *Hawaii Mars* (C-FLYL) and *Philippine Mars* (C-FLYK). Each drop can cover an area of four acres. As can be expected, it is difficult to join the pool of pilots; the basic minimum is 5,000 hours on water-based aircraft on the coast of the province. The crew consists of a captain, first officer and two flight engineers. Both aircraft are currently at their long-term base at Sproat Lake, Port Alberni, Vancouver Island, but are not in operational use. As late as 2016, one of the aircraft made an appearance at the EAA (Experimental Aircraft Association) Air Venture show at Oshkosh, Wisconsin, operating from the nearby Lake Winnebago.

Boeing B-17F Flying Fortress N17W c/n 4896 Tanker 04, operated by Aircraft Specialities of Mesa, Arizona, is on station at Porterville, California, in October 1979. It was sold to the Boeing Museum of Flight, Seattle, in September 1990 and is kept in an airworthy condition.

Boeing B-17F N17W takes off at Abbotsford, British Colombia, in August 1986.

Boeing B-17G N5237V c/n 32509 Tanker 65 is operated by TBM Inc at Dinuba-Sequoia Field, California, in October 1979. It is now preserved at the RAF Museum at Hendon, UK.

Boeing B-17G N3702G c/n 9613 Tanker 61 is operated by TBM Inc at Dinuba-Sequoia in October 1979. It is now preserved at the Castle Air Museum, California, marked as *Virgins Delight*.

Boeing B-17G N9563Z c/n 32204 Tanker 89 is operated by Aircraft Specialities at Mesa, Arizona, in October 1979. It is now with the Lyon Air Museum at Santa Ana/John Wayne Airport, California, and flies as *Fuddy Duddy*.

Boeing B-17G N9323R c/n 8737 Tanker 37 is operated by Aircraft Specialities in October 1979. It is now preserved at the Pima Air & Space Museum, Tucson, Arizona, as *I'll be around*.

Boeing B-17G N3193G c/n 8738 Tanker 34 is operated by Aircraft Specialities, in October 1979. It now flies with the Yankee Air Museum, Willow Run, Michigan, as *Yankee Lady*.

Boeing B-17G N3509G c/n 8687 Tanker 102 is operated by Western Air Contractors of Utah. It is at Porterville, California, in October 1979. It is now with the Palm Springs Air Museum, California, as *Miss Angela*.

Boeing B-17G N207EV c/n 32426 Tanker 22 is operated by Evergreen Aviation at Marana, Arizona, in October 1979. It was restored as a warbird and displayed at the Evergreen Museum at McMinnville, Oregon, as *Shady Lady*. In August 2015, it was sold to the Collins Foundation to fly again.

Grumman F7F-3 Tigercat N7654C c/n C-115 Tanker 63 is operated by TBM Inc at Dinuba-Sequoia in October 1979. It is now on show at the US Navy Museum, Pensacola, Florida.

Grumman F7F-3P Tigercat N7235C c/n C-167 Tanker 64 is operated by TBM Inc at Dinuba-Sequoia in October 1979. It was sold on and is now N909TC and flies in US Marine Corps markings as a warbird.

Grumman F7F-3N Tigercat N7629C c/n C-116 Tanker 41 is operated by Sis-Q Flying Service at Santa Rosa, California, in October 1979. Sold on, it now flies as a warbird in a US Navy scheme from Chino, California.

Grumman TBM-3E Avenger N9590Z c/n 4638 Tanker 25 is operated by Aircraft Specialities at Mesa in October 1979. Since then, it has had several owners, a forced landing in 1986, a rebuild, and, as of 1996, it was flying again is US Navy markings.

Grumman TBM-3E Avenger N6447C c/n 3637 is operated by Craig Aero Services at Shafter Field, California, in October 1979. It is now with the Lone Star Flight Museum, Galveston, Texas.

Grumman TBM-3R Avenger N9927Z c/n 2688 Tanker 39 is operated by Aircraft Specialities at Mesa in October 1979. It is now operated as a warbird in France as F-AZJA.

Left: Grumman AF-2S Guardian N9995Z c/n 269 Tanker 21 was retired at Chico, California, at the end of the 1973 fire season. It is pictured there in October 1984. It was later donated to the EAA (Experimental Aircraft Association) Foundation at Oshkosh, Wisconsin, and was present at their 1986 show; it is now with a private owner in Texas.

Below: Lockheed PV-2D Harpoon N83L c/n 15-1501 of Dothan Aviation at Wheeless Field, Dothan, Alabama, in October 1981. It was later restored and flown out as a warbird in July 1991.

Lockheed PV-2 Harpoon N7086C c/n 15-1410 Tanker 112, formally of T&G Aviation, at Chandler, Arizona, in September 1988. It was last reported derelict at this location in 2018.

Consolidated PB4Y-2 Privateer N3739G ex-59819 Tanker 30 of T&G is pictured at the company base at Chandler in October 1984. In 1991, it moved to the Lone Star Flight Museum, then in Galveston, and was damaged by saltwater flooding in 2008 during Hurricane Ike. Its restoration to flight was abandoned, and it moved to the Pima Air & Space Museum in 2015.

Privateer N3739G on the move at Chico in September 1988, whilst on station as a water bomber.

PB4Y-2 Privateer N2872G ex-66300 Tanker 124 of Hawkins and Powers Aviation (H&P) on station at Fox Field, Lancaster, California, in October 1979. H&P operated it from 1969 to 2006 when it moved to the Yanks Air Museum at Chino, California.

PB4Y-2 Privateer N6884C ex-59701 Tanker 127 of H&P on station at Douglas County Airport, Nevada, in September 1988. It was operated by the company from 1970 to 2006 and is currently parked at Greybull, Wyoming, on loan to the Museum of Flight and Aerial Fire Fighting.

PB4Y-2 Privateer N6884C on station at Fox Field in October 2001.

PB4Y-2 Privateer N6884C departs Santa Barbara, California, after a refuelling stop in October 2001.

Consolidated PBY-5A Canso (Catalina) C-FFFA c/n 1886 Tanker 7 of Flying Fireman. It is at their Sidney, British Colombia, base in September 1984. They operated it from 1977 to 1988. It is now airworthy with the Erikson Aircraft Collection at Madras, Oregon, in a US Navy scheme.

PBY-5A Canso C-GFFH c/n 2008 Tanker 8 of Flying Fireman at their Sidney base in September 1984. It was sold as EC-EVK to SAESA (Servicios Aereos Espanoles SA) in Spain.

PBY-5A Canso EC-EVK c/n 2008 is operated by SAESA at Cuatro Vientos, Madrid, in September 2002. It was later sold to the Qantas Foundation Memorial at Longreach, Queensland, as VH-EAX in September 2009. It now wears period BOAC markings as 'G-AGIE' and is named *Antares Star*.

PBY-5A Canso C-FPQM c/n CV425 Tanker 714, operated by Buffalo Air, is pictured at Red Deer, Alberta, in May 2000. It was sold to Exploits Valley Air Services, Gander, Newfoundland, in 2013.

PBY-5A Canso C-FOFI c/n CV343 Tanker 703 of Buffalo Air at Red Deer in August 2005. It was sold to a new owner in Buckeye, Arizona, as N413PB in 2007.

PBY-5A Canso CF-UAW c/n CV201 Tanker 708 of Buffalo Air at Hay River, Northwest Territories, in September 2008. It was sold the following year to Pacific Flying Boats, Victoria, British Colombia, and flies in RCAF livery with the name *Shady Lady*.

The Warbirds

A pair of PBY Cansos of Buffalo Air are pictured at Red Deer in August 2005.

A line of six Douglas A-26C Invaders of Conair Aviation awaits winter storage at their Abbotsford base in September 1984.

A-26C Invader C-FKBZ c/n 29031 Tanker 27 of Conair Aviation at Abbotsford in September 1984. This aircraft was operated by Conair from 1973 to 1988. It was sold to the Canadian Warplane Heritage at Hamilton, Ontario, in 1988 and is now with the Carolinas Aviation Museum, Charlotte, North Carolina, as N81797.

A-26C Invader C-FKBM c/n 27415 Tanker 20 of Conair Aviation at Abbotsford in September 1984 in a bare metal finish. It was sold to Air Spray (1967) Ltd the following year.

A-26C Invader N9425Z c/n 29000 Tanker 57 of Lynch Flying Tankers at their Billings, Montana, base in August 1986. This aircraft featured in the film *Always*. It was sold to Bob Pond as a warbird in 1992.

A-26C Invader N4805E c/n 27400 Tanker 58 of Lynch Flying Tankers at Billings in August 1986. It was sold to a private owner in Seattle during 1992.

A-26C Invader C-FOVC c/n 28776 Tanker 56 of Air Spray at their Red Deer base in May 2000. It was sold to a private owner in Alberta during 2014.

A-26C Invader C-FOVC c/n 28776 Tanker 56 of Air Spray heads a line at Red Deer in September 2008.

Above: A-26C Invader C-FPGP c/n 29177 Tanker 2 of Air Spray runs its engines to do an oil burn check at Red Deer in August 2005. It was sold and flown to Australia the following year and is now registered as VH-VNI.

Right: A line of six Invaders is pictured at Red Deer in September 2008.

Below: A line of three Invaders is pictured at Red Deer in May 2000.

Martin JRM-3 Mars C-FLYK c/n 9264 *Philippine Mars* of Forest Industries Flying Tankers (FIFT) at its Sproat Lake, Vancouver Island, base in September 1984. It was later owned by Coulson Flying Tankers and was due to be sold to the US Navy Museum in 2012, but the sale was blocked by the Canadian Government Heritage Act.

JRM-3 Mars C-FLYL c/n 9267 *Hawaii Mars* of FIFT pictured at Sproat Lake in September 1984.

JRM-3 Mars C-FLYL is pictured out of the water at its Sproat Lake base, receiving maintenance in May 2000.

Of a similar look to the Boeing Stearman, one of the smallest water bombers was the Naval Aircraft Factory N3N-3 N45084 ex-4497 fitted with a 450hp P&W R-1340 Wasp radial. Pictured hanging from the hangar roof at Chico in September 1984, it operated between 1957 and 1964. The Jensen on the fuselage is for Charlie T Jensen, who traded as Farm Air of Sacramento, California, and other company names. It is now preserved at the Pima Air & Space Museum.

Chapter 4
Post-War Pistons

First flown in May 1945, the Lockheed P2V Neptune was a long-range maritime patrol aircraft for the US Navy. The prototype was powered by a pair of Wright R-3350 radial piston engines of 2,300hp; on later versions, this had increased to 3,500hp, and a pair of 3,400lb st Westinghouse J-34 turbojets had been added under the wings. It served until April 1978, when the last USN reserve patrol squadron retired the type. The Neptune also served with many other air arms around the world.

The late 1960s saw the US Forest Service test a water bomber conversion of this aircraft, and, during the following decade, a number of companies operated the type. Two of the companies doing the actual tanker conversions had different results. Aero Union of Chico, California, had a smooth aerodynamic finish with a 2,000-gallon tank almost flush into the lower fuselage. The under-wing jets had been removed for the new role, but they retained the MAD (Magnetic Anomaly Detector) tail boom from its maritime patrol days. The prototype converted aircraft was known as an Aero Union Firestar and was registered in 1986.

Down in the southwest of the US in Alamogordo, New Mexico, Black Hills Aviation (which had been formed in 1964 in South Dakota, hence the name, and moved to New Mexico in 1971) also converted Neptunes. Their variant had a 2,700-gallon, six-door tank, which was far more pronounced under the fuselage. They removed the MAD boon but retained the jet engines under the wings. In 1993, Black Hills was sold to Neptune Aviation Services and moved to its new base at Missoula, Montana. The Neptune remained in service with them until 2017, when the seven aircraft in the fleet were retired and found new homes in museums around the nation.

Additionally, there were proposals to re-engine the Neptune with turboprops, but this never came about. It is of note that the Japanese Maritime Self Defence Force operated a turboprop variant as early as 1966. The engine used was the General Electric T-64, built under licence in Japan, with a power output of 2,850shp.

All three of the Douglas four-engined airliners have found a role in the world of water bombers. First of the type was the DC-4; it was first flown in February 1942 at Santa Monica, California. Most of the early production was the military C-54 and, post-World War Two, the civil DC-4. The engines for the type were 1,450hp P&W R-2000 radial pistons. As with the Neptune, several different companies have made conversions. Aero Union again made a very aerodynamic one and would convert aircraft for other companies, as well as for themselves. The aircraft fitted with the RALCO tank were noticeable for their angular shape. Both tank conversions held 2,000 gallons. The DC-4/C-54 could be found in limited use into the 2000s.

First taking to the air in February 1946, the Douglas DC-6 was one of the finest piston-engined airliners of its day. They can still be found in service today as cargo and bulk fuel tanker aircraft in Alaska. The DC-6 was used by a number of operators of water bombers, and the size of the tank would vary depending upon the conversion, but the capacity was in the range of 2,400 to 3,000 gallons. The DC-6 and its military version, the C-118, were powered by four P&W R-2800 radial pistons with an output of 2,500hp each.

The last shall be first. It was by accident that the largest of the four-engine DC airliners, the DC-7, became a water bomber. In the summer of 1953, the prototype N301AA was on a test flight when the crew dumped 1,300 gallons of water ballast over the airport at Palm Springs. The result was a swathe, some 200ft wide and almost a mile long. Later that year, the Los Angeles County Fire Department conducted a number of tests. The aircraft was fitted with six 400-gallon tanks, making a load of 2,400 gallons, fed through nozzles, rather than tanks with doors. The location of the tests was Rosamund Dry Lake in California. The tests were successful, but the project went no further, as, at that time, the DC-7 was a very expensive 'state-of-the-art' airliner, and it would not be sound economics to have them sitting on a ramp on the off chance that a fire would start. However, 20 years later, large piston engine airliners were largely out of passenger service and airframes could be bought at budget prices. Converted, the aircraft could carry a load of 3,000 gallons in a tank under the fuselage. The powerplants for the DC-7 were Wright R-3350 radial pistons of 3,250hp each. The last DC-7 water bomber was not retired until October 2020, when Erickson Aero Tanker flew DC-7B N838D c/n 45347 to its base at Madras, Oregon. The aircraft is to be kept in flying condition, in case the need for its services should happen again.

It would seem to be that the most logical airframe to be converted would be a dedicated designed cargo aircraft, as these aircraft have a large empty area to fit the tanks. This has not always been the case, and some cargo aircraft conversions have not been successful. One such was the Fairchild C-82 Packet, which carried a 2,000-gallon load for spray use in the 1950s. The type was a twin-boom transport with a box-like fuselage. It first flew in 1944 and entered military service two years later with the USAAF. Power came from a pair of P&W R-2800 radial pistons with an output of 2,100hp. It was not a success, however, as it was underpowered.

The C-82 was developed into the far larger C-119 Boxcar with the same twin-boom layout. Powerplants were a pair of Wright R-3350 radial pistons of 3,500hp, and later models had a pair of General Electric J-85 turbojets, one under each wing, with an output of 2,850lb st. Some of the water bomber conversions had just a single jet mounted above the fuselage, as well as the two piston engines. A load of 2,400 gallons could be carried with the jet boost, without it the load was 1,800 gallons. When not in use for firefighting, there was enough room in the fuselage for a useful load of cargo. One of the main users of the C-119 was Hemet Valley Flying Service based at Hemet, California. The company started firefighting operations in 1957; they purchased the fleet of C-119s in 1974 and operated them until 1987, when they were withdrawn because of safety concerns. The company ceased all operations in 1996. Another user of the C-119 was Hawkins and Powers of Greybull, Wyoming, which had bought a number of ex-Royal Canadian Air Force airframes, but not all were converted, and some remained in store at Greybull or for use as spares.

Developed from the Chase XG-20 cargo glider, the Fairchild C-123 Provider had two P&W R-2800 radial pistons with an output of 2,300hp each. The C-123K, a later variant, had a pair of GE J-85 turbojets of 2,850lb st. During the Vietnam War, 34 of this variant were fitted with under-wing spray bars and redesignated UC-123K. Their role was to fly over the dense Vietnamese jungle, spraying the highly toxic Agent Orange to defoliate the trees and deny the Vietcong the cover of the forest. This chemical damaged the health of both the USAF crews handling it, as well as the victims it was sprayed upon. California-based TBM Inc purchased three airframes in the early 1980s for conversion to water bomber status. Only one aircraft was fitted out with a 2,000-gallon tank in 1982. It spent several years operated by Hemet Valley Flying Service, but 1990 saw it preserved in the Pima County Air Museum, Tucson, Arizona, in a section of retired water bombers.

Another type that had only one aircraft converted to the role was the Boeing C-97 Stratofreighter. It had first flown in November 1944 as a transport aircraft, but its most widespread use was that of an in-flight refuelling tanker for the USAF, with nearly 600 aircraft built as KC-97Gs. In 1964, some of the airframes allocated to the US Air National Guard were fitted with a GE J-47 turbojet under each wing with an output of 5,200lb st; this added to the type's four 3,500hp P&W R-4360 radial pistons and helped make up the speed difference as they refuelled fighter jets. This variant was known as the KC-97L and it served until 1977. From this stock, a number of aircraft were acquired for use as water bombers and were to be fitted with a 3,000-gallon tank; however, only a single airframe was converted. This was done by Hemet Valley Flying Service in 1982, which then leased it to Hawkins and Powers from 1985 to 1991. It is currently in store at Greybull.

One of the longest service lives for a water bomber type is the Grumman S-2 Tracker. It first flew in December 1952, entering service in February 1954 in the role of carrier-borne anti-submarine aircraft. More than 1,200 airframes were built and a further 100 licensed produced by de Havilland Canada for that nation's navy. It also served with the air arms of 13 other nations as far apart as Japan and Uruguay. The year 1970 saw the first conversions in Canada by Field Aviation for the Ontario Ministry of Natural Resources. Following the success of this, a further 11 were converted. Also in Canada, during 1978, Conair of Abbotsford, British Columbia, began to convert what has become one of the most popular versions, the Conair Firecat. To convert the airframe, all the surplus military equipment is removed and in its place is a flush fitting 870-gallon tank with four doors so the pilot can control how much is dropped on each pass over the fire area. In the US, various operators have made conversions, and with the number of available retired airframes, there is no shortage of extra aircraft or spare parts.

To extend the life of the Tracker, many have been re-engined to turboprop power. In many places, there is a shortage of aviation gasoline (AVGAS) for use in piston-powered aircraft, whilst aviation turbine fuel (AVTUR) is far more freely available and usually much cheaper. The first such change was made by Marsh Aviation of Mesa, Arizona, at the end of 1986, and it was based at Fresno in the central valley of California during 1988, under test by the CDF. The original pair of Wright R-1829 radial pistons of 1,525hp were replaced by two Garrett TPE331 turboprops with an output of 1,250shp driving a five-blade propeller that replaced the earlier three-blade one. Conair have produced the Turbo Firecat, this having a P&W Canada PT-6A engine with an output of 1,424shp. One of the many modifications made during conversion to Firecat was to increase the size of the main wheels, as the originals were not always ideally suited to some of the small remote sites that the fleet are dispersed to during the summer fire season. The size of the undercarriage doors had to be increased to facilitate this. The aircraft are flown by a single pilot and have a fatigue life of 12,000 hours. As well as their own fleet, Conair have supplied Firecats to France's Sécurité Civile, which had the turbine conversion done by Conair. All of their fleet made the long trip to Canada's west coast as piston-powered aircraft and came back to France, following the re-engine work, as turboprops.

Each of the provincial governments of Canada have their own water bomber fleets; the lumber industry is an important part of the nation's economy and has to be protected. In the province of Saskatchewan, the headquarters for aerial firefighting is at La Ronge in the north of the vast province. They have their own smart white and green livery on the fleet. As the season ends, they will begin maintenance on the aircraft. For the Trackers, the wings are removed for non-destructive testing, the engines are removed for service and the undercarriage is overhauled. At La Ronge, there is a certified avionics workshop, together with an extensive holding of spare parts, many of which are no longer in production. During the summer season, they operate from bases at Buffalo Narrows, Prince Albert, Meadow Lake, Hudson Bay, Baker Narrows, and Stony Rapids, as well as La Ronge. On occasions when the risk is low and other provinces have large fires, they may be asked to deploy to assist; they have been as far west as British Colombia and as far east as Newfoundland. On operations, they will drop the retardant from about 140ft above the trees but may fly as low as 30ft at a speed in the region of 105kts. They will not drop onto the actual flames but put the retardant ahead of the direction the fire is moving. This can create an area for the fire to burn itself out.

From their headquarters in the state capital of Sacramento, at the former McClellan AFB, Cal Fire operate a fleet of more than 20 turbine powered Trackers. Each summer, usually in the month of May, they will disperse to the 13 bases around the state they operate from. In the past, the season ran until late October, but with the current change in climate, the season may be extended at both ends of the calendar. The advantages of the turbine-powered Tracker include the cost of fuel, better single engine performance, more power at hot and high bases and a quieter engine to put less strain upon the single pilot. The aircraft has an endurance of 4.5 hours and a range of 500 miles when loaded, or 800 when empty.

Lockheed SP-2E Neptune N203EV c/n 5228 Tanker 142 of Evergreen Aviation is at Marana, Arizona, in October 1984. It had been converted to a tanker that year, and it was withdrawn from use in 2000 and sold to Neptune Air Services in 2010.

EP-2E Neptune N126Z c/n 5044 Tanker 1 of the US Forestry Service (USFS) is pictured at Marana in October 1979. It had been converted in 1970 by Rosenbalm Aviation in Oregon for evaluation by the USFS and was withdrawn in 1979. It was purchased by Evergreen Aviation in 1984 and broken up for spare parts for their fleet.

SP-2H Neptune N4235T c/n 726-7285 Tanker 09 of Blackhills Aviation is pictured at its then base in Alamogordo, New Mexico, in October 1984.

SP-2H Neptune N4235T c/n 726-7285 Tanker 09, now with Neptune Aviation, on station at Fox Field in October 2006. It crashed in September 2008 after take-off from Reno Stead Airport, Nevada, when the left-hand jet failed and caused it to roll to the left and impact the ground. This had fatal results for the three crew on board.

P2V-7 Neptune N14447 c/n 826-8010 Tanker 11 of Blackhills Aviation is pictured at Alamogordo in October 1984.

P2V-7 Neptune N14447 c/n 826-8010 Tanker 11, now with Neptune Aviation, running its engines at Lancaster in October 2006. It crashed in June 2012 north of Modena, Utah, during a fire attack mission. A wing tip collided with terrain, followed by a yaw to the right and impact with the ground; both crew members died.

P2V-7 Neptune N65170 c/n 826-8025 Tanker 08 of Blackhills Aviation at Florence Municipal Airport, Arizona, in October 1979. It had been converted to a tanker in 1972 and it crashed in September 1990 near Wynoochee Dam, Washington, whilst firefighting in Olympic National Forest. The fire had been caused by the crash of a Cessna 172. After dropping its retardant, it impacted terrain during the pull-up. The two crew members did not survive.

SP-2H Neptune N443NA c/n 726-7168 Tanker 43 of Neptune Aviation at Fox Field in October 2006. It was withdrawn from use in September 2017 and delivered for preservation to the San Diego Air & Space Museum at their storage base at Gillespie Field in September 2018.

Above: Two Neptunes of Neptune Aviation are pictured on standby at Fox Field in October 2006.

Left: A trio of Neptune tails of Neptune Aviation on standby at Fox Field in October 2006. Note the different livery on the one in the middle.

Below: SP-2H Neptune N299MA c/n 726-7211 Tanker 99 of Minden Air at Avra Valley Airport, Arizona, in October 1998. It crashed in October 2003 at East Highlands, California, whilst on a ferry flight. It impacted terrain when in cloud, and both crew members died. The company were based at Minden Airport, Nevada, and ceased trading in September 2016.

SP-2H Neptune N718AU c/n 726-7214 Tanker 18 of Aero Union at their Chico base in October 2001. It was sold to Bravo Airlines of Opa Locka, Florida, in 2007.

SP-2H Neptune N80232 c/n 726-7198 of Maricopa Aircraft Services is pictured at Avra Valley Airport in September 2007. It had been partially converted to a tanker during 1991 and was struck off the US civil register in March 2018.

Grumman US-2A Tracker N436DF c/n 052 Tanker 100, owned by the CDF (California Department of Forestry) and operated by Hemet Valley Flying Service from 1978 to 1984, is pictured at Fresno, California, in October 1979. It crashed whilst firefighting near Monterey, California, in September 1984.

US-2B Tracker N404DF c/n 455 Tanker 80, owned by the CDF and operated by Hemet Valley Flying Service, is pictured at their base of Hemet Airfield, California, in September 1988. They operated it from 1988 to 1992, and it was struck off the US civil register at the end of 2014.

CS2F-1 Tracker C-GHQY c/n DHC-35 Tanker 62 of Conair Aviation is pictured at their Abbotsford base in September 1984. This Canadian-built airframe had been converted to a Firecat in April 1979, and it crashed near McBride, British Colombia, in August 1986.

CS2F-2 Tracker C-GABC c/n DHC-90 Tanker 67 of Conair Aviation at Abbotsford in September 1984. It had been converted to a Firecat in March of the previous year and was withdrawn from use after the 2012 season. It is now preserved at the Reynolds-Alberta Museum at Wetaskiwin.

Six of Conair's Firecats are pictured in a line at Abbotsford in September 1984.

With the season over, Conair's Firecats are seen back at Abbotsford in September 2008 for winter storage. Note the discs covering the engine intakes.

The Grumman Tracker was built in large numbers, so there was a ready stock of airframes for conversion to water bombers or for spare parts. Pictured at Fresno in October 1979 is a store of unconverted aircraft.

US-2A tracker N420DF c/n 388 Tanker 75 of the CDF, operated by San Joaquin Air of Delano, California, is pictured at Paso Robles, California, in October 2001. It was withdrawn from use in 2006 and sold to a private buyer.

Right: TS-2S Tracker N406DF c/n 293 Tanker 95 of the CDF is pictured at the former McClelland AFB, California, in October 2006. It had been withdrawn from use and was later sold to a private buyer in that state.

Below: Upon retirement of the piston-engined fleet of Trackers, these aircraft spent some time at McClelland before they were disposed of. This line of three was photographed in May 2006.

Opposite, above and below: CS2F-2 Tracker C-GEHR c/n DHC-51 Tanker 503 is operated by the Province of Saskatchewan. First it warms its engine, then takes off, makes a low pass and then drops water on a test flight at La Ronge, Saskatchewan, in September 2008. It had been converted to a tanker in 1976 and was later withdrawn from use and then struck off the Canadian register in 2017.

CS2F-2 Tracker C-GEQE c/n DHC-92 Tanker 506, operated by the Province of Saskatchewan, receives maintenance at the unit's base of La Ronge in September 2008. It had been converted to a tanker in 1976 and was withdrawn from use at Abbotsford in 2014 and struck off the Canadian register two years later.

TS-2A Turbo Tracker N426DF c/n 522 Tanker 180 is owned by the CDF and is pictured in evening light at Fresno in September 1988. It had been converted by Marsh Aviation of Mesa in November 1986 and was operated by Hemet Valley Flying Service from 1988 to 1993. It was the first re-engined Tracker being tested that year. It later went back to Marsh Aviation and was re-registered as N613MA.

Marsh (Grumman) S-2T Turbo Tracker N746MA c/n 655 Tanker 155 of March Aviation is pictured at its Mesa base in October 1998. In its history, it had served with both the US and Japanese navies and was converted as the first production Marsh S-2T in 1996.

US-2A Turbo Tracker F-ZBAA c/n 027 Tanker T22 of the French Sécurité Civile is pictured at Cazaux in the southwest of France in June 2005. It had been converted to a Conair Firecat in 1987 and then a Turbo Firecat in 1993. It crashed while firefighting at Generac, France, in August 2019.

Above: Pre-season, before they disperse to their summer bases, six S-2T Turbo Trackers of the CDF line up at their McClelland base in May 2009.

Left and below: Marsh S-2T Turbo Tracker N431DF c/n 109C Tanker 78 is pictured in the current smart Cal Fire livery at Ramona, California, in May 2019.

S-2T Turbo Tracker N436DF c/n 224C Tanker 76 of Cal Fire is on station at Porterville in May 2019.

An S-2T Turbo Tracker tanker and an OV-10 Bronco lead aircraft await the call to arms at Porterville in May 2019.

S-2T Turbo Tracker N442DF c/n 295C Tanker 94 of Cal Fire is pictured ready for action at Porterville in May 2019. Note that under the cockpit window is the base name, Redding. Early in the season, some aircraft may be sent to bases with a higher risk of fire before the aircraft scheduled for Porterville is ready. They will usually swap around to have the correct aircraft at the correct base as soon as possible.

Left: Three S-2T Turbo Tracker tankers of Cal Fire line up in front of the company hangar at McClelland in May 2019.

Below: S-2T Turbo Tracker N437DF c/n 0865-004 Tanker 73 of Cal Fire awaits its season at the Hemet-Ryan base. It is pictured at McClelland in May 2019.

S-2T Turbo Tracker N442DF c/n 295C Tanker 84 of Cal Fire is back at McClelland following a short deployment at Porterville and awaits its journey to Redding for the summer fire season.

Right: Under maintenance at McClelland, in May 2019, is S-2T turbo Tracker N425DF c/n 294C Tanker 89. It is the aircraft for the base at Grass Valley. Note, for ease of maintenance in the hangar, the wing folding ability from its days with the USN on board aircraft carriers had been retained.

Below: Fairchild C-119C Boxcar N13746 c/n 10389 Tanker 87 of Hemet Valley Flying Service is on station at Paso Robles in October 1979. Hemet operated it between 1974 and 1992, and this aircraft is now preserved at the museum at Dover AFB, Delaware.

C-119C Boxcar N13742 c/n 10431 Tanker 88 of Hemet Valley Flying Service is at Santa Barbara in October 1979. In July 1981, it crashed at Los Padres National Forest when the wing structure failed; the two crew did not survive.

C-119C Boxcar N13743 c/n 10369 Tanker 81 of Hemet Valley Flying Service is pictured at the company base of Hemet Valley in September 1988. This aircraft is now preserved at the Pima Air & Space Museum as an air tanker.

A pair of C-119s of Hemet Valley Flying Service are pictured at Hemet Valley in September 1988. Note the difference in the livery between the two aircraft.

C-119G Boxcar N15501 c/n 10955 Tanker 01 of Hawkins and Powers is at its base of Greybull in August 1986. They operated it between 1976 and 2005. During this time, it flew to Namibia to appear in the remake of the film *Flight of the Phoenix*. It has been sold several times since 2005 and was last reported at Buckeye. It was struck off the US civil register in 2019.

Water Bombers

C-119G N8091 c/n 10906 is unconverted as a tanker and is being worked on by Hawkins and Powers at Greybull in August 1986. Two years later, it was preserved at the March Field Air Museum at March AFB, California.

Boeing KC-97L N1365N c/n 16729 Tanker 84, the sole one of its type to be converted, is at Greybull in August 1986. Owned by Hawkins and Powers, it was leased to Hemet Valley Flying Service from 1985 to 1991.

Post-War Pistons

Boeing KC-97L N1365N c/n 16729, now Tanker 97, is pictured upon its arrival for the summer at Fort Wainwright, Alaska, in May 2000. It was back being operated by Hawkins and Powers at the time of photographing and is currently in store at Greybull.

Fairchild C-123K Provider N3142D c/n 20029 Tanker 63 of TBM Inc is on station at Stockton, California, in September 1988. It was the sole conversion of the type in 1982. It has been preserved at the Pima Air & Space Museum since 1990.

Water Bombers

Douglas C-54 Skymaster N82FA c/n 35960 Tanker 161, owned by Aero Flite of Kingman, Arizona, is on duty at Chico in October 2001. It was sold to Brooks Air Fuel of Fairbanks, Alaska, in 2006.

C-54 N11712 c/n 3088 Tanker 02 of Aero Union is on station at Hemet Valley in September 1988. They operated this aircraft from 1977 to 2000, when it was sold to Buffalo Airways in Canada.

C-54 N62342 c/n 10613 Tanker 13 of Aero Union is on station at the Porterville base in October 1984. It was sold to Buffalo Airways in Canada at the end of 2005.

C-54 N76AU c/n 10547 Tanker 16 of Aero Union is on station at Fox Field in October 1984. They bought the aircraft in 1976, retired it in 1990 and sold it to Aero Flite in 2001, where it was re-registered as N3054V.

C-54 N4989P c/n 36082 Tanker 19 of Aero Union is pictured at the Hemet Valley Air Attack Base in September 1988. It crashed in June 1995 near Ramona, California, following a mid-air collision with a USFS Beech 58P Baron N156Z as they approached to land.

C-54 N8502R c/n 27367 Tanker 165 is owned by Kenneth Spiva and is pictured at Stockton in October 1984. It had been converted to a water bomber in 1981, with a tank designed by Waig Aircraft Inc and was sold to TBM Inc in February 1987. It had been operated for the previous three years by ARDCO (Aerial Retardant Delivery Company) of Ryan Field, Tucson, Arizona.

C-54 N8502R c/n 27367, now Tanker 65, is owned by TBM Inc and is pictured at their base of Dinuba-Sequoia Field in May 2006. It was sold to Brooks Air Fuel, but they ceased operation and it never joined their fleet. It was last reported as in store at Wendover, Utah, in 2019.

Below and opposite above: C-54 N9015Q c/n 22178 Tanker 152 of ARDCO on guard at the USFS Air Attack Base at Fox Field in October 2001. A few days later, it is pictured taking off from Santa Barbara. It was sold to Air Elite Corp of Texas in 2008.

Below: **C-54 N406WA** c/n 35944 Tanker 119 of ARDCO at the company base of Ryan Field in September 1988. They had purchased the aircraft in 1981, and, in December 2001, they sold it to Florida Air Transport for general cargo operations.

C-54 C-FIQM c/n 36088 Tanker 57 of Buffalo Airways is pictured at their southern base at Red Deer in May 2000. They had purchase it from Aero Union in August 1988.

C-54 C-FBAP c/n 36089 Tanker 15 of Buffalo Airways is pictured at Hay River in September 2008. It had been bought from Aero Union three years earlier and is still in their basic livery.

Post-War Pistons

C-54 C-FBAJ c/n 3088 Tanker 02 of Buffalo Airways is at Hay River in September 2008. It had been bought, like a lot of their fleet, from Aero Union and is the former N11712 pictured earlier.

A trio of Buffalo Airways C-54s are pictured at Hay River in September 2008.

C-54 N96454 c/n 10864 Tanker 105 of Maricopa, Arizona-based Central Air Services is pictured at Porterville in September 1988. They had bought the aircraft in 1981 and sold it ten years later. It was later withdrawn from use at Rantoul, Kansas.

C-54 N96451 c/n 10592 Tanker 111 of Central Air Services is pictured at Tucson International Airport in September 1988. It was sold in April 1991.

Douglas DC-6B F-ZBAE c/n 43834 Tanker 63 of the French Sécurité Civile is at Paris Le Bourget in May 1983. It crashed near Perpignan, France, in April 1985 when it struck a rocky cliff in thick fog; all five on board died.

DC-6B F-ZBBU c/n 45219 Tanker 64 of the Sécurité Civile is at Paris Le Bourget in May 1983. It crashed on the eastern slopes of the Puig Llobregat Mountain in July 1986 whilst fighting a wasteland fire near Cantallops, Spain; all four crew members died.

DC-6B N888SQ c/n 43562 Tanker 48 of Sis-Q Flying Service at Wenatchee-Pangborn, Washington, in September 1984. The company was purchased and renamed Macavia the following year, and this aircraft was sold to T&G in 1991.

DC-6 N90MA c/n 43128 Tanker 21 of Sis-Q Flying Service is pictured on duty at Chico in October 1984. It was sold on and scrapped at Chandler.

DC-6B N555SQ c/n 45137 Tanker 45 of Sis-Q Flying Service is at the company base of Santa Rosa in October 1979. It was sold in 2004 to Everts Air in Alaska.

DC-6 N90739 c/n 43044 Tanker 97 of TBM Inc is pictured at Fresno in October 1984. It was scrapped in May 2007.

DC-6B N80MA c/n 43127 Tanker 20, operated by Macavia International Corporation, has its engines turning at Chico in September 1988. It was sold to T&G in 1991 and later to a company in Africa.

DC-6B C-GHCB c/n 44893 Tanker 43 of Conair being worked upon at the company's Abbotsford base in September 1984. Note how the retardant spills and marks the concrete as the aircraft is being cleaned. This airframe was withdrawn from use in 2001 and later scrapped.

DC-6B C-GHCA c/n 45197 Tanker 44 of Conair is at their Abbotsford base in September 1984. They operated it for ten more years before it was withdrawn from use and later scrapped.

DC-6B C-GICD c/n 45496 Tanker 47 of Conair is at their Abbotsford base in September 1984. It was sold to Everts Air Fuels of Alaska in 1996 and became N151. In June 2020, it was flown to Norway as LN-SUB and is now preserved at the Flyhistorisk Museum, Sola, and wears the markings of the airline Braathens SAFE, which operated it during the 1960s.

DC-6B C-GHLY c/n 45501 Tanker 46 wears the updated livery of Conair at Abbotsford in August 2005. It was sold to Everts Air Cargo in 2013 and was re-registered as N501ZS; it is now in store.

DC-6A/C C-GIBS c/n 45531 Tanker 51 of Conair is at Abbotsford in September 2008. They had purchased the aircraft in 1982 and sold it to Everts Air Cargo in 2013, and it was re-registered as N501YP. It is now in store.

Douglas DC-7B N4887C c/n 45351 Tanker 33 of T&G/International Air Response (IAR) is pictured at Fox Field in October 1984.

The same DC-7B N4887C, with the same company but in a new smart livery, at Palmer, Alaska, in May 2000. This aircraft is now preserved at the Delta Flight Museum, Atlanta, Georgia.

DC-7C N90802 c/n 45112 Tanker 115 of T&G/IAR at the company base of Chandler in October 1984. It was sold as EC-GGB in 1995 to Spanish operator BASAER (Baquero Servicios Aéreos), which operated for ICONA, the administrative unit of the government that looked after the natural environment. It was later scrapped, and the cockpit section is in the Musée Européen de l'Aviation at Montelimar-Ancone, France.

DC-7B N838D c/n 45347 Tanker 60 of TBM Inc is at Fresno in October 1979. It was sold to Erickson Aero Tanker and not withdrawn from use until October 2020. It was the last DC-7 water bomber in service.

DC-7B N848D c/n 45454 Tanker 61 of TBM Inc is at Stockton on fire protection duty in September 1988. It crashed whilst firefighting in October 1992 near Union Valley Reservoir, California, when it impacted high ground, killing both crew members.

DC-7C N9734Z c/n 45215 Tanker 32 of T&G is at Billings in August 1986. It was sold to BASAER in Spain as EC-GGC in 1995 and was withdrawn from use around 2000. It is now preserved at the Parque de Miraflores, Cordoba.

Chapter 5
Turboprops

The Lockheed C-130 Hercules first flew in August 1954 and is still in production today; a record of 67 years for any transport aircraft. Of course, over these many years, it has been improved, but the basic outline of the aircraft still looks the same. The bulk of the users have been the air forces of the world, and, as newer versions were produced, the early C-130As, powered by four 3,750shp Allison T-56A turboprops, have been withdrawn from military use. A number of 'A' models were acquired by civilian operators for conversion to water bombers, being fitted with 4,000-gallon tanks. They have not been as widely used as expected, as there have been several fatal crashes due to a failure of the structure and the wing breaking away whilst fighting fires. Later models, however, are now in wider use. Cal Fire are in the process of converting at least three airframes of C-130H models at its Sacramento-McClellan base to full tankers in their attractive colour scheme. Canada's Coulson Aviation operates a variant fitted with their own designed 4,000-gallon Coulson RADS-XXL roll-on roll-off tanker system.

When the federal, state or private contractors are at full stretch during a busy fire season, there is one more organisation that can be called upon to assist. It is the US Air Force, in the form of the Air Force Reserve Command (AFRC) or the Air National Guard (ANG). They will bring in C-130 transport aircraft, which will have been fitted inside with, on a pallet, MAFFS (Modular Airborne Fire Fighting System). It was the FMC Corporation of California that designed, built and tested the modular tank that enabled a basic C-130 to be converted in a couple of hours. The tank has a capacity of 2,700 gallons. To operate the rear ramp, loading doors had to be opened for the two high-capacity hoses to discharge the retardant or water. The system was first tested at Edwards AFB, California, in July 1971.

MAFFS II is an upgrade of the system, featuring a slightly larger tank of 3,000 gallons. In this version, the outlet is now a door on the left side normally used for parachute drops; the whole door is quickly replaced by one with the single nozzle built into it, which can be set for different rates of dispersal. It also enables the aircraft to remain pressurised, and, as this version does not require having the rear ramp open, drag is reduced on the airframe, thus improving the performance. The first test of MAFFS II was in 2007, with operations the following summer.

As can be imagined, the crews for this challenging operation need special training for the role, and, within an ANG or AFRC unit, only a selected few are put through the training for the skills needed; recruits must have several years on C-130s before they can even fly as first officer on the fire-bombing missions. To qualify as an aircraft commander, the pilot must have flown two fire seasons and have performed no fewer than 15 live drops on a real fire as first officer. To be an instructor pilot for MAFFS flights, the pilot needs to have worked for four fire seasons and made at least 60 live drops on an actual fire. This is all in addition to their normal qualifications for standard C-130 cargo and parachute operations, including low and formation flying.

As well as the flight deck crew, the system is under the control of two loadmasters who are able to control the output of the retardant. They can dump the full load of 3,000 gallons at one drop, or it can be divided into fractions of a half, a third or a sixth. They can also control the actual amount of coverage from four to eight gallons per square foot, with six being the most usual. The military crews are directed by the Fire Boss and will follow a smaller aircraft, such as a Beech King Air, across the path on which they are to drop the load. ANG units from the states of Nevada, California and Wyoming are MAFFS trained, as well as an AFRC unit in Colorado; all four units have two aircraft each for MAFFS fitting and need to have ten crews trained for the role. All these states have large amounts of forest. Up to eight C-130s, including the latest 'J' models, are available, as required, from the ANG and AFRC units trained in the MAFFS system. The MAFFS Corporation is a combination owned by the United Aeronautical Corp and Blue Aerospace. The MAFFS equipment is owned by the US Forest Service, and the costs of the military aircraft are borne by the agency responsible for the area of forest that is burning.

In 1943, Vultee Aircraft merged with Consolidated Aircraft to form Consolidated Vultee, and, in 1947, this was shortened to Convair. With World War Two over, they wanted to build a new airliner and, in 1946, produced the Convair 110. However, this was considered too small by the airline customers so the 240 followed (two engines, 40 passengers). It was piston-powered with a pair of P&W R-2800 radial engines with an output of 2,400hp each. From this model, the Convair 340 and 440 were developed. These airframes were able to be updated by the replacement of the piston engines with 3,750shp Allison 501 turboprops. The work was done by Pac-Aero, with the first of many being converted in 1960. The designation for the re-engined aircraft was Convair 580.

The type has found favour in Canada as a water bomber. The design authority for the type has been taken over by Kelowna Flightcraft, and they worked with Conair of Abbotsford, which designed and fitted the retardant tank holding 2,000 gallons; both companies are situated in the province of British Colombia. The Conair tank has a computer-driven digital control system, and this enables the aircraft commander to control the level and quantity of the retardant dropped, thus producing the required pattern.

At the end of 2010, Conair flew two aircraft to Australia for a three-month trial during the southern hemisphere summer. They were based at Avalon in the state of Victoria, which had requested the tests. Western Canada to Australia is a long journey and involved 38 flying hours. The route was from Abbotsford to Oakland, California, then on to Honolulu, Hawaii, Majuro, in the Marshall Islands, Cairns, Queensland, and then down the coast to Avalon. Conair are in the process of replacing the CV580 over the next few years with the de Havilland Canada DHC-8-Q400 Dash-8.

Across Canada, the Province of Saskatchewan operates the Convair 580 from their headquarters at La Ronge in the north. One of their fleet had, in a previous life, carried that most famous of call signs – 'Air Force One'. In its USAF days, it was built as a C-131D, but, in 1966, it was converted to a turboprop and redesignated a VC-131H (the 'V' was for VIP). In October 1972, it flew then President Richard Nixon to Huntington, West Virginia, an airport too small for the usual jets. Any aircraft that has the current US president on board has the right to use the Air Force One call sign. As well as the president, it was used a lot by the Vice President Gerald R Ford; the call sign is then 'Air Force Two'.

After evaluating a number of aircraft types, Conair selected the DHC-8-Q400 for its next generation of turboprop water bombers. The first modified was in 2005, and they have flown more than 8,000 hours since then. There are two versions of the aircraft, one is the Q400MRE multi-role and the other is the Q400AT air tanker. Both have the same external 2,642-gallon tank. They are in service in France with the Sécurité Civile. The multi-role version is capable of a quick conversion from air tanker to a cargo, passenger, medevac or combi configuration. The aircraft is powered by a pair of 5,000shp P&W PW150A turboprops and can cruise fully loaded at 360kts, slow to 125kts to drop its retardant and operate from a 5,000ft runway.

The Lockheed L-188 Electra first took to the air in December 1957 from the company's Burbank, California, factory. It was a four-engine passenger airliner powered by 3,750shp Allison 501 turboprops; the launch customer for the type was Florida-based Eastern Air Lines. Two events cast a shadow over it. One was the arrival of the pure jets, and the travelling public did not want to see an aircraft with propellers, despite it being the state-of-the-art for the time. The other was far more serious; it was a series of fatal accidents in which the aircraft broke up in flight. The cause was eventually traced to excess vibration leading to a wing root failure. Lockheed designed a cure for this, and all aircraft were modified. The type had a long life in second-tier airlines, with the last passenger-configured ones flying in Alaska. They are still flying as cargo aircraft based in Yellowknife, Canada; it is also in this vast nation that water bomber Electras can be found. Air Spray, based at Red Deer, Alberta, pioneered the role and its aircraft are equipped with a 3,000-gallon tank. Air Spray have named the type Longliner.

Developed from the Electra, the Lockheed P-3 Orion is a maritime patrol aircraft that was ordered by the US Navy to replace its fleet of Lockheed P-2 Neptunes. The first one flew in November 1959 and entered service in 1962 with Patrol Squadron Eight (VP-8). It is still in USN service, albeit much updated, as well as the air arms of more than a dozen other nations. As newer variants joined the USN, older P-3A models were released and Aero Union of Chico, California, had a fleet of eight P-3A Orions that it named Aerostars. As well as operating water bombers, it was in the forefront of both the design and manufacture of retardant tanks, as well as the conversion of the aircraft; like the Electra, the converted Orion had a 3,000-gallon tank. They entered service with the company in the early 1990s, working on contracts from the USFS. When the aircraft were on a base, the flight crews worked a six-day week with up to 14 hours in any one day. Actual flying time was limited to eight hours in one day, to a maximum of 42 hours in a seven-day period. Since some contracts could last for six months or more, relief crews were needed to cover pilots going on holiday.

In May 2011, Aero Union ceased all operations unexpectedly. The reason for this was a Federal Aviation Authority (FAA) audit that claimed it had not performed a mandatory structural fatigue inspection. The company had had a contract to supply six Aerostar tankers worth US$30m, but this was then cancelled by the USFS. Negotiations to continue service failed, so the company filed for bankruptcy, with several hundred staff finding themselves out of work. November 2013 saw the fleet sold to United Aeronautical Corporation, with one later joining Buffalo Airways. They now fly, still in the very smart livery of Aero Union, for Airstrike Firefighters LLC, a company with bases in Alaska and California but now carrying the title 'Airstrike' on the fuselage.

One of the goals of aircraft companies during the mid-1950s to 1960s was to design and build the so-called 'Dakota replacement'. Some were more successful than others, and the real Dakota replacement has proved to be another Dakota, as it is still in passenger service, albeit limited, to this day. In terms of numbers built, the Dutch Fokker F.27 Friendship has sold the most. It first flew in November 1955, and the launch customer was the Irish flag carrier Aer Lingus, which began operations at the end of 1958. The aircraft was powered by a pair of Rolls-Royce Dart turboprops. The first water bomber conversion was by Conair in the mid-1980s. It was fitted with a 1,680-gallon tank fitted under the fuselage, and the aircraft's pressurisation system was removed to avoid complications. It went on trial to the Sécurité Civile in France but was sadly written off in a fatal crash in September 1989. Since then, at least two others have been converted and operated in France.

In the vast land mass that made up the former USSR, much of it is forests, and the summers in the far north have many hours of daylight and sunshine, leading to dry areas and the risk of forest fires. Since there are few, if any, roads in these areas, a conventional fire engine cannot be used and so fires need to be attacked from the air. One of the types converted for the role was the Antonov An-32. This was the final variant of the An-24, and it has nearly twice the power of the original type. It is fitted with a pair of 5,180shp Ivchenko AI-20M turboprops. So big are the propellers needed for this that the engines are mounted above the wing to give the airscrews sufficient ground clearance. Based in Kiev (now Kyiv),

Ukraine, the Antonov Design Bureau (OKB) designed and fitted four tanks, which were in pairs on the sides of the fuselage. They are not removable and dispense the water, the usual load, through a series of flaps. They can carry 2,100 gallons. This system means that the cargo hold of the aircraft is untouched and can be used for equipment when going to remote bases or even to drop firefighters by parachute. This model is known as the An-32P Firekiller. The prototype of the variant first flew early in 1993, and, following flight and drop tests, some work was needed to solve problems that had occurred. It was tested for real in Spain and Portugal during 1994 and has been ordered by the Ukrainian Ministry of Emergency Situations.

Lockheed L-188A Electra C-FQYB c/n 1063 Tanker 88, operated by Air Spray, is pictured at the company base of Red Deer in May 2000. It was destroyed in a hangar fire at this location in October that year.

L-188A Electra C-FLJO c/n 1103 Tanker 482 of Air Spray is at their Red Deer base in September 2008. It was delivered to them in 2006 and is still current.

Lockheed P-3A Orion N921AU c/n 185-5098 Tanker 21 of Aero Union is pictured at the company base of Chico in October 2001. It had been converted to an Aerostar tanker in 1992. The company ceased operations in May 2011, and it was sold to Airstrike Firefighters LLC in 2013.

P-3A Orion N900AU c/n 185-5014 Tanker 00 of Aero Union is at their Chico base in October 2001. It had been converted to an Aerostar tanker in 1991–92 and was sold to United Aeronautical Corporation, North Hollywood, California.

P-3A Orion N922AU c/n 185-5100 Tanker 22 of Aero Union takes off from Santa Barbara in October 2001. It had been converted to an Aerostar in 1992–93 and sold to Buffalo Airways USA and was on lease to Airstrike Firefighters during the 2020 season.

The bright red of the Aero Union livery on this pair of P-3 Orions contrasts with the blue Californian sky at Chico in October 2001.

Above: Fokker F.27 Friendship C-GSFS c/n 10473 Tanker 27 of Conair is at Abbotsford in August 1986. It was leased to the Sécurité Civile in France and crashed in September 1989 whilst firefighting at Laval-Pradel. It descended too low and impacted trees; both crew members died.

Left: F.27 Friendship C-GSFS is pictured dropping a load at Abbotsford in August 1986.

Convair 580 C-FHKF c/n 374 Tanker 55 of Conair is at its Abbotsford base in August 2005. It had been converted to a tanker in 2000 and is still current with the company.

Convair 580 C-FKFA c/n 100 Tanker 52 of Conair runs up both its engines at Abbotsford in August 2005. It is still current with the company.

Convair 580 C-GSKR c/n 509 Tanker 471 is operated by the Province of Saskatchewan at their La Ronge base in September 2008. It had been delivered to them in 2006 and is still current.

Convair 580 C-GSKQ c/n 217 Tanker 475 is operated by the Province of Saskatchewan and is at their base at La Ronge in September 2008. Whist serving with the USAF as a VIP transport, it flew the US President Richard Nixon to an airport in West Virginia and so was able to use the call sign 'Air Force One'. It had been delivered to the water bombing unit earlier that year and is still current.

Three of Saskatchewan's Convair 580s line up at La Ronge in September 2008.

De Havilland Canada DHC-8-Q400AT C-FFQF c/n 4315 Tanker 540 of Conair is on duty at Palmer, Alaska, in July 2021. This is the new type that Conair plan to replace their Convair 580 fleet with. Note the bulge in the fuselage where the tank is fitted. (Photo by Ian Atkinson)

Right: Antonov An-32P Firekiller UR-48086 c/n 2901 is owned by the Antonov Design Bureau (OKB) and is pictured at Moscow-Zhukovsky in August 1995. Note the bulges on the fuselage where the water tank has been fitted.

Below: An-32P Firekiller UR-48086 drops water at Moscow-Zhukovsky in August 1995. This aircraft is now with Constanta Airlines and has been reregistered as UR-UZH.

Lockheed C-130A Hercules N473TM c/n IA-3081 Tanker 63 of TBM Inc is at Dinuba-Sequoia Field in October 2001. In May 2019, it was in store at Castle Airport, California, missing one engine and a set of propellers.

C-130A Hercules N117TG c/n IA-3018 Tanker 81 of IAR is pictured at Chandler in October 1998. It had been converted in 1993 by Aero Union and used in France from 1993 to 1995. It is currently used by IAR for oil spill duties.

C-130A Hercules N116TG c/n IA-3086 Tanker 82 of IAR is at Chandler in October 1998. It crashed in September 2000 whilst with the Sécurité Civile during a firefighting mission, when it flew into a hill northwest of Aubenas, France.

C-130A Hercules N138FF c/n 382-3227 Tanker 88 of IAR is pictured at Chandler in October 1998. It was re-registered as N119TG and was substantially damaged following an emergency landing at Santa Barbara in August 2019 following a ground loop and fire.

C-130E Hercules 61-2359 c/n 382-3651, operated by the 146th Tactical Air Wing, California Air National Guard. It has '4' on it in Day-Glo and is a MAFFS I-equipped firefighter. It is pictured on duty at Stockton in September 1988 and is now in store at Davis-Monthan AFB, Tucson.

Left: C-130H Hercules 94-7317 c/n 382-5391, operated by 731st Air Sqn 302nd Air Wing Air Force Reserve Command. It is a MAFFS II-equipped aircraft and pictured at Oshkosh in July 2009. It is still active with the US military.

Below left: A close-up of the MAFFS II retardant loading valve.

Below right: The MAFFS II retardant discharge valve. Note that the whole door unit is replaced when this is fitted.

C-130H Hercules N130FF c/n 382-4901 Tanker 131 of Coulson Aviation. It is on duty at Porterville in May 2019 and is marked 'Next Gen Airtanker'.

The air tanker line-up at Porterville in May 2019.

EC-130Q Hercules N134CG c/n 382-4904 Tanker 134 of Coulson Aviation is on the move at McClelland in May 2019. This aircraft crashed in January 2020 near Cooma, New South Wales, Australia, whilst firefighting. It impacted terrain and all three crew members died. It had been converted to a tanker by 2017.

HC-130H Hercules N116Z c/n 382-5002 Tanker 116 of the USFS. It is pictured at McClelland in May 2019 and still has the serial 1708 from its days with the US Coast Guard. Since then, it had been repainted in the attractive Cal Fire colour scheme.

Chapter 6

Jets

For airlines, the biggest costs, after the aircraft themselves, is the fuel they burn. This has an unwelcome habit of going up in price, and any saving that they can make is welcome to them. For major carriers, if a new airliner or variant of an existing one is introduced, they will often place orders for it if it will promise a few per cent savings on the fuel burn. A few per cent might not sound like a lot, but over a fleet of several hundred aircraft flying each day, it adds up to millions of pounds or dollars per year. So, what happens to the older airframes? Some will have reached the natural end of their lives and be scrapped; others will be parted out for spares as the value of all the parts that can be reclaimed and sold on is, in some cases, worth more than the complete aircraft. Depending upon the type, the airframe may be converted to a cargo aircraft or find use in local airlines in third-world nations. For a small, but growing, number, they may find a new role as a water bomber.

One of the first and the most successful jet operators is 10 Tanker STC. They now operate a fleet of four McDonnell Douglas DC-10-30 aircraft, which are powered by three GE CF-6-50 engines with an output of 51,800lb st. This size of aircraft places it in the 'Very Large Air Tanker' (VLAT) category. Under the fuselage are three tanks for the retardant. The front and rear ones hold 2,700 gallons, and the centre one has a capacity of 4,000 gallons, making a total of 9,400. It is able to empty the entire load in four seconds and can vary the coverage level through ten different levels. Drops are made 200–300ft above ground level at a speed of 140kts; en route to the fire from its base, it will cruise at between 300kts and 350kts. On board is a crew of three: captain, first officer and a flight engineer, whose task is to operate the aircraft's systems and set the required drop rate. As this is written, the company has flown more than 900 missions to more than 130 fires and dropped nearly nine million gallons, making 2021 a very busy season so far. The retardant weights 9lb per gallon, whilst water comes in at 8.3lb per gallon. For a 9,400-gallon tank, this is a difference of 6,580lb. However, the normal load is retardant and the weight of this is 84,600lb. With a full load, the DC-10-30 will carry fuel for 2.5 hours.

The company originally flight tested a DC-10-10 version in May 2003. This aircraft had a single tank under the fuselage that could hold 12,000 gallons of water. On the ramp, it could refill the tank in just eight minutes. When using water for the original proof of concept, it had a flow rate of up to 1,500 gallons per second to achieve the coverage requested by the firefighters.

The other VLAT was the Boeing 747-200. Originally developed by Evergreen International Aviation, it was tested as a water bomber in 2004 but did not get any contracts and the aircraft was returned to cargo configuration. A second try was made with a 747-100, and it toured Europe in 2009 and even tackled a fire in Spain. A few short-term contracts were flown over the next few years, but the company was declared bankrupt in 2013. The assets were purchased by Global SuperTanker Services, which converted a 747-400 and operated it for a number of years before operations ceased early in 2021 and the aircraft returned to cargo configuration.

When is a water bomber not a water bomber? The answer is if it is a Russian Ilyushin IL-76. The reason for this is any IL-76 can be converted into the role in a few short hours. All they need to do is open the tail ramp and load in the VAP-2 tanks. These are twin cylindrical tanks that can hold 11,000 gallons of water. The IL-76 is a Russian heavy lift freighter in service with their air force as well as a number of others including India, North Korea, Cuba and Syria, as well as civil operators. It first flew in March 1971, and, following development work and service trials during 1974, production began the following year at Tashkent. Powerplants for the type were four Soloviev D-30KP jets with an output of 26,400lb st. Tests of the water bomber role commenced in the late 1980s.

Compared with some systems, the IL-76 could perhaps be called low-tech – but it works, and with a fire burning, that is all that matters. Being a military freighter, the aircraft has a 20-wheel undercarriage that distributes its weight so the footprint is quite light for its size. Also, it can operate with a full load from a 6,000ft runway, depending upon the airfield's height and temperature. When over the fire, the tail ramp is opened, a slight nose up attitude is adopted, the VAP-2 tanks are opened either both at once or singularly, and gravity does the rest: the water cascades down out of the ramp onto the fire. Retardant can be used, if available. With water, it just needs eight to ten seconds to empty the tanks, whilst if it is retardant then 15 to 20 seconds are needed. When both tanks are opened, it will douse an area 1,800ft long by 325ft wide, and if one tank is opened at a time then the area expands to 3,950ft by 295ft.

It has been demonstrated in Europe and Australia with the plan for nations to contract the aircraft and the Russian crew, rather than purchasing one of their own. During demonstrations, the USFS have witnessed this but, as yet, there have been no contracts for the US. The aircraft have operated in Chile, and, in 1999, the Greek government contracted the IL-76 for the summer high-risk season from the middle of June until the end of August. During that period, over 1,000 tons of water were dropped during 25 missions. In August 2021, the type was in operation in Turkey.

In a class of its own is Russia's Beriev Be-200, as it is the only new-build, purpose-designed jet water bomber. It was a scaled-down version of the Beriev A-40 Albatros maritime patrol amphibian, coming in at around half the weight. The design work started in 1989, and it first flew ten years later in September 1998. The following year, it flew for the first time from water. The engines are a pair of Progress D-436TP turbofans with an output of 16,500lb st. This version of the engine is the maritime variant and is corrosion resistant. They are mounted high to avoid water ingestion during take-offs and landings. To take off on land, a runway of 5,900ft is needed, whilst at sea 7,500ft clear is required, with the water being at least 8ft deep.

It is a sea skimming aircraft that will speed along the water, either a lake or the open sea, at 90 to 95 per cent of take-off speed to fill its tanks. There are eight of these under the cabin floor with a capacity of 3,200 gallons. There are four retractable water scoops, two forward and two aft of the fuselage step, and they can fill the tanks in 14 seconds with 12 tonnes of water. If operated from a land base, the tanks can be filled by any truck or water supply. When it comes to drop its water, it can either dump the whole load in one go or as eight single units, one from each tank.

In its home country of Russia, it is used by the Ministry of Emergency Situations, which has supplied aircraft and crews for both demonstrations and actual firefighting. One of the first was in 2004, when the Protezione Civile contracted the Be-200 for use on the Italian island of Sardinia. It was so successful that it returned the following year. Other nations have also used the type, including Portugal in 2006 and 2007, Greece in 2007, Indonesia in 2007 and in 2015, Israel in 2010, Serbia in 2013 and 2014, and Turkey in 2021. The first foreign sale was in 2008 to Azerbaijan. Other sales include China, with two firm orders and two options in 2017, Chile with two, and the biggest foreign sale was in 2018 to US-based Seaplane Global Air Services, which ordered four, with six options. The Be-200 would have to be certified by the FAA before operations could take place in the continental US.

As mentioned in the introduction to this section, some airliners have fallen out of favour with airlines due to newer types having far better fuel consumption. Since water bombers fly a lot less than airliners, only operating when there is a fire or for test flights to keep the pilots current if there are no real fires to fight, higher fuel burn is not a problem. Another reason the aircraft may be converted is the cost to acquire the airframe has dropped, owing to normal commercial carriers not wanting them. One such is the McDonnell Douglas MD-87. It was a direct development from the original Douglas DC-9, which first flew in 1965; it was 21 years later that the first MD-87 flew, and they can still be found in airliner service. Erickson Aero Tanker of Hillsboro, Oregon, started MD-87 operations in 2014 and now have a fleet of five operational aircraft with two more airframes unconverted. The MD-87 has a 3,000-gallon tank inside the fuselage, and, in the early days of operations, the retardant outlets were flush with the belly of the aircraft. However, there were the odd instances of retardant being ingested into the rear-mounted engines. To cure this, the company fabricated and fitted an external pod below the tank's doors. This lowered the release point by 46in, thus solving the problem. To load the retardant there is a 3in nozzle forward of the wing and the loading time is seven minutes with an average of 450 gallons per minute. The MD-87 needs a runway length of 5,000ft and can land fully loaded. This fact is important, as if the drop is cancelled, then the retardant does not have to be wasted to bring the aircraft down to a safe landing weight. The MD-87 can cruise to a fire at 450kts whilst the actual drop is at 135kts to 140kts. It may look odd, but the undercarriage is lowered for dropping. This is an FAA requirement to prevent the aircraft stalling. When the drop is completed, the aircraft can climb to altitude; as they fly pressurised, this means a saving on fuel and time to return to base to reload for another drop. One of the advantages of the jets is that they are fast, so international travel is possible in a relatively short time frame. Two of the fleet flew to Australia to assist the government for their southern hemisphere summer season at the end of 2019 and into 2020.

Coulson Aviation of British Colombia have been involved in forest protection for some years, and they have been the lead company in using the early models of the Boeing 737. They purchased six 300 series airframes from Texas-based Southwest Airlines and have fitted them with a 4,000-gallon tank and named the new version Fireliner. The first one was used in Australia in late 2018 with the New South Wales Rural Fire Service to such success that they have actually ordered three, so they will have them all year round and not just during the Australian summer.

The last of the jet water bombers looks like it will be the most successful in terms of numbers converted. It is the British Aerospace BAe 146 -200/RJ-85. This aircraft is a regional jet powered by four Avco Lycoming (later Allied Signal) ALF504 turbofans. The first company to start looking at the type in the new role was Minden Air Corp, Minden, Nevada, as far back as 2001. By 2004, a 146-100 version, owned by Tronos of Canada and flown by a BAe test pilot and a Minden pilot, proved the concept of the type by flying fire attack profiles. Work started on one of Minden's two 146-200s. By 2014, it had reached full conversion and was tested at Fox Field, Lancaster, California. This test was to measure the quantity and uniformity of the retardant drop pattern; it involved 3,000 cups on poles above the ground, which are then measured after the flight to see how much is in each cup. Tests first used water and then retardant. The company had a cash flow problem and ceased all services, and the converted and second unconverted airframes are in store at the company base. The first aircraft, N446MA, had its registration cancelled in March 2018.

It was far better news from Neptune Aviation of Missoula, Montana. They were a customer of the system developed by Tronos, which featured tanks inside the fuselage, pressurised, to release the retardant through four nozzles, situated behind the main undercarriage, in the aircraft's belly. This was not perfect, so a later modification called REV-3 added two extra nozzles forward of the undercarriage as a retrofit. Tronos tested the aircraft at their base on Canada's east coast in 2009. May 2011 saw the first delivery to Neptune, which put it into immediate service. It was that summer that the USFS cancelled contracts with a number of operators, leaving the forests of the US with much-reduced fire cover. To help resolve this, Neptune was given approval in the interim to operate the 146 and got their first contract that year. They now have a fleet of nine aircraft and carry a 3,000-gallon tank. They also have 'call when needed' contracts with the states of California and Minnesota.

Canadian company Air Spray took over the hangar of Aero Union in 2014 and have operated the 146 since 2018. The aircraft are fitted with Air Spray's own internal computerised variable flow IRADS tank with a capacity of 3,000 gallons. The aircraft can cruise fully loaded at 330kts and will drop retardant between 125kts to 140kts. It has an endurance of 4.5 hours and can operate from a gravel strip and be ready to take off from a cold start in just three minutes.

Conair is one of the longest established water bomber operators. As well as this role, they also design and build the tanks and convert the aircraft to their new roles. Their work on the 146 is quite different from the other ones, as it has a conformal underbelly tank wrapped around the lower part of the fuselage. It has a capacity of 3,000 gallons and Conair have converted the later variant of the 146: the BAe RJ 85. This is the same size as the 146-200 used by the other companies. It is in service with Conair themselves as well as Spokane, Washington-based Aero-Flite. This operator used to be at Kingman, Arizona, but moved north in 2014. One of their contracts was to go to Australia. British Aerospace has been involved in the 146 water bomber programme from the very start and has provided technical expertise to the companies doing the conversions and has even flown, in the UK, profiles of typical fire attack patterns to help feed information to the convertors.

McDonnell Douglas DC-10-10 N450AX c/n 46942 Tanker 910, operated by 10 Tanker Air Carrier, is at US Marine Corps Base Miramar, California, in October 2006. The company has put this aircraft into storage at Oscoda-Wurtsmith, Michigan, as they now use the DC-10-30 model.

DC-10-10 N450AX is pictured at Paris Le Bourget in June 2005. Note how little ground clearance there is under the belly tank. It then drops water.

Beriev Be-200ES RF-21512 c/n 7682000003 is operated by the Beriev Aircraft Company. It is pictured on the ramp at Al Ain, UAE, in January 2007. It later joined Russia's Ministry of Emergency Situations.

Above and below: Be-200ES RF-21512 shows off its elegant lines at Al Ain in January 2007. Note the high mounted engines; this is to stop water ingress when landing or taking off on water. It then drops a tank of water.

Ilyushin IL-76TD RA-76845 c/n 1043420696 is at Moscow-Zhukovsky in August 1995. It is operated by the Ministry of Emergency Situations. The title on the nose is in the Russian Cyrillic alphabet, and the first three letters are the abbreviation for the ministry and the second word is 'Russia'. The long grey pipes situated between the two IL-76s are the VAP-2 water tanks for converting it into a water bomber.

IL-76TD RA-76429 c/n 1043419639 operated by Russia's Ministry of Emergency Situations is demonstrating a water drop at the Austrian airshow at Zeltweg in July 2000. It is still current with the ministry. (Photo by Steve Williams)

McDonnell Douglas MD-87 N291EA c/n 53039 Tanker 101 operated by Erikson Aero Tanker of Madras, Oregon, is on duty at Fox Field in May 2019.

A pair of Erickson MD-87s are pictured ready for action at Fox Field in May 2019.

MD-87 N219EA is ready with the door open. Note that it has its own integral set of steps as well as ventral stairs under the tail.

The interior of the MD-87 water bomber showing the two holding tanks for the retardant. Since the crew are at bases for some time, they do need a place to hang their clean clothes!

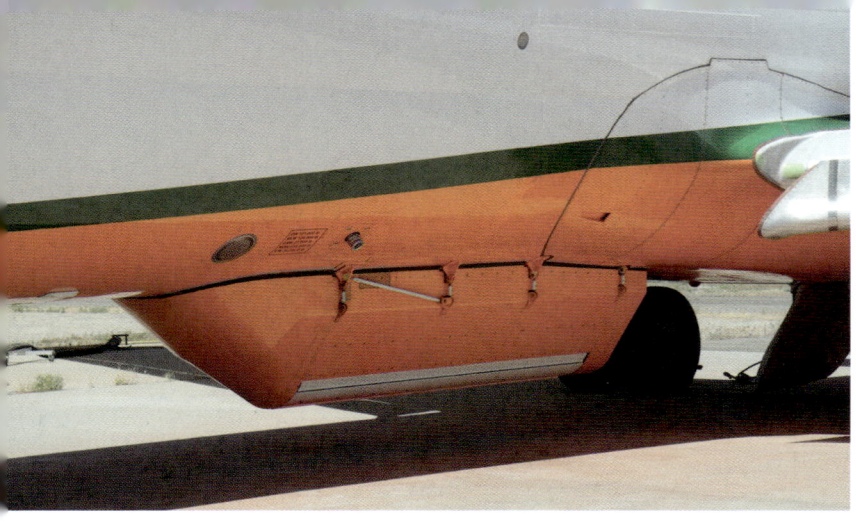

Left: A close-up of the MD-87s external pod below the tank doors. This lowered the release point of the retardant by 46in and solved the problem of the occasional ingestion of retardant into the rear mounted engines.

Below and bottom: British Aerospace BAe 146-200 N476NA c/n E2196 Tanker 12 is operated by Neptune Aviation Services of Missoula, Montana. It is pictured at Oshkosh in August 2019. (Photos by Steve Williams)

Chapter 7
Purpose-Built Water Bombers

It was the fact that Canada's vast lumber industry needed protection from forest fires that drove the nation to be the first to design and build, from scratch, a purpose-built water bombing aircraft. In the latter part of 1963, a symposium of forest protection fire officers and operators came together to discuss the ideal aircraft for the role. Canadair, following the recommendations of that meeting, designed the CL-215. It was to be an amphibious flying boat powered by a pair of 2,100hp P&W R-2800 radial piston engines; a well-proven unit, it also powered types like the Douglas DC-6.

The CL-215 had a 1,600-gallon tank, which could be filled in any one of three ways: (1) with retardant at an airfield base, the method most used in the US; (2) for retardant to be mixed with water scooped up; (3) and the last method was for the aircraft to skim across a lake, of which there are many in Canada, to lower retractable scoops to collect water. A run of 4,000ft in ten seconds will fill the tanks. Dropping can be done at one dump or as a number of separate ones, depending upon the requirements of the fire chief. On a single drop, an area 350ft long by 40ft wide can be covered.

The prototype CL-215 first took to the air in October 1967 and made its first water landings and take-offs in May the following year. In Canada, each of the different provinces look after their own firefighting and are able to finance the purchase of new, expensive, purpose-built aircraft with possible low utilisation depending upon the number of fires in the area. For a commercial company, the acquisition of new aircraft would be too expensive. Of course, these companies still get contracts, but they use older aircraft that have been written down in book value over the years as they depreciate; in some cases, the aircraft has, over time, been written down to zero book value.

Despite the costs of new aircraft, the provinces have still reported cost benefits, as the value of the lumber saved outweighs the unit's operating costs. The CL-215 is a very productive aircraft, as proved by one in Quebec Province that made 31 pick-ups and drops in a one-hour period. It may be assumed that the fire was close to a lake. Operations during summer usually involve two aircraft and a spotter dispersed across the province to a number of bases; the aircraft will be on call seven days a week during daylight hours. A look at a map of Canada will show all the major cities are in the south of the country near the US border, whilst vast areas of the nation have a sparse population. The province of Ontario is 66 per cent covered in forest with around 85 billion trees.

At the Dryden, Ontario, base there is some high-tech equipment to help predict where there might be a fire. It is a lightning counter, which plots on a map all the strikes that occur over a period of 24 hours. It is colour co-ordinated to show the time period and specific areas that are receiving a lot of strikes, and there can be thousands over a large area, which can be marked as at high risk and watched. All the aircraft carry a three-number code, and most of the CL-215s fleets are painted bright yellow so they can be easily seen. One exception to this is aircraft from Saskatchewan, which operates in a white scheme with green trim. As the cost of AVGAS rose to unacceptable levels for budgets, and, more importantly, its availability, some of the remote outposts developed a plan to re-engine the CL-215s with turboprops or replace the whole fleet with the newly built CL-415. The second-hand ones coming onto the market were often bought by the commercial operators, with Air Spray being the first non-government operator of the type. As well as the Canadian provinces, the CL-214 has been sold to governments and air arms around the world including Croatia, France, Italy, Spain, Greece, Portugal and Turkey. In Venezuela, they have a dual use, being both a water bomber and a transport aircraft seating 26 passengers. The navy in Thailand use it as a maritime patrol aircraft, with a secondary role as a water bomber.

First built by Canadair (later Bombardier), the CL-415 was the second-generation aircraft, designed to replace the CL-214. However, in 2016, the production and design authority rights were sold to Viking Aircraft of British Colombia, which now produces the type. The powerplants for the CL-415 are a pair of P&W (Canada) PWC-123AF turboprops with an output of 2,380shp. As well as new engines, it features a more up-to-date glass cockpit, and the first flight was in December 1993. Its role is the same as the water skimming scooping. The tank can hold 1,621 gallons of water, which can be scooped up in 12 seconds. The tank has various door settings to suit the needs of the fire. It can be identified by the fact that both the elevators and wing tips have extra editions fitted to them.

In France, the Sécurité Civile are a major user of the CL-415, having also operated the CL-215. The French pilots have fewer lakes than their Canadian counterparts and, therefore, use the open sea, usually the Mediterranean, for their water supply. Before taking on this task, pilots will begin training on a flat lake before open-sea scooping and are always under the instruction of an experienced captain.

Left: Canadair CL-215 C-GOFO c/n 1102 Tanker 226, operated by the Aviation and Fire Management Centre of the Ministry of Natural Resources of Ontario. It is pictured at Thunder Bay, Ontario, in June 1990. It was sold to the Minnesota Department of Natural Resources Aviation Center as N226NR and operated for them by Aero Flite.

Below: CL-215 C-GENU c/n 1082 Tanker 263 has both engines running at Dryden, Ontario, in June 1990. It is operated by the Province of Ontario and was sold to Minnesota as N263NR.

Purpose-Built Water Bombers

CL-215 C-GDRS c/n 1081 Tanker 262 is at Dryden in June 1990. Then operated by the Province of Ontario, it, like several others, was sold to Minnesota and is now N262NR.

A pair of Ontario's CL-215s share the ramp at Dryden in June 1990.

CL-215 C-GUMW c/n 1065 Tanker 251 operated by the Province of Manitoba is pictured at Winnipeg in September 2008.

Back from their summer seasons, a trio of Manitoba CL-215s share the ramp at Winnipeg in September 2008.

CL-215 C-GFSL c/n 1086 Tanker 202 is operated by the Province of Alberta and is pictured at Abbotsford in September 2008. In 2010, it was converted to turbine power and was in service with Conair by 2014.

CL-215 C-GFSK c/n 1085 Tanker 201, operated by the Province of Alberta, is pictured at Red Deer in May 2000. It was converted to turbine power in 2014 for this operator.

CL-215 C-GBYU c/n 1083 Tanker 290 is at Yellow Knife, Northwest Territories, in September 2008. It was operated by the Forest Management Division of Northwest Territories. It has since been converted to turbine power.

CL-215 C-FAFO c/n 1094 Tanker 217, operated by the Province of Saskatchewan, is at La Ronge in September 2008. It has since been converted to turbine power and is current with this operator.

A line of four Saskatchewan CL-215s are pictured at La Ronge in September 2008. They are about to begin their time in winter storage. It is of note that this province has their aircraft painted white with green trim, whilst most others are always yellow.

CL-215 C-FTUW c/n 1030 Tanker 208 is operated by Air Spray at their Red Deer base in September 2008. The company claimed to be the first non-government operator of the type.

CL-215 C-GDHN c/n 1089 Tanker 296 is operated by Buffalo Airways and leased from the NWT Forest Management Division. It is at Red Deer in May 2000.

Above and left: CL-215 1039 c/n 1039 is operated by 355 MTM (Squadron) of the Elliniki (Hellinic) Polimiki Aeroporia (Greek Air Force). Based at Elefsis, they have operated the type since 1974. It is pictured on approach to Athens Airport in June 1993.

Below: Canadair CL-415 I-DPCF c/n 2059 Tanker 23 of the Italian government's Protezione Civile. It is pictured at Luqa, Malta, in September 2004.

Top, above and right: CL-415 I-DPCF is pictured flying and dropping water at Luqa in September 2004.

CL-415 F-ZBFY c/n 2010 Tanker 35 of France's Sécurité Civile at Armée de l'Air (French Air Force) base, BA 120 Cazaux, in June 2005. It then drops water.

Chapter 8
Single-Engine Types

In recent years, the light single-engine water bomber has made a comeback. The earlier World War Two types, such as the Grumman Avenger and Guardian, had been banned by the authorities in the US. However, the new types are mostly turboprops and vastly more reliable. One of the most widely used is the Air Tractor AT-802. Built in Olney, Texas, the type's most common role is as an agricultural spray plane, but the company also produce, as a land plane, a water bomber variant. It has an 800-gallon tank and is powered by the well proven P&W Canada PT-6A-67F turboprop with an output of 1,600shp. It was a development from the AT-502 crop duster. The company markets an extra use of the aircraft for forest restoration following a fire by using the tank for reseeding the burnt area.

The more popular version, the Air Tractor AT-802F Fire Boss, a scooping amphibius air tanker, was created by an alliance between two companies, Air Tractor and Fire Boss LLC. Air Tractor builds the airframes and makes all the modifications needed and then it goes to Fire Boss, which adds the scooping floats. Fire Boss is based in St Paul, Minnesota, and is part of the Wipaire Group, which make aircraft floats. Wipaire started on the project in 2001, and it was their Wipline 10000 scooping float, joined to the AT-802, that produced the Fire Boss variant. More than 100 are in operation in Europe, Asia, Australia, North America, and South America, where it is used by the National Police of Colombia, as well as operators in Chile.

Fire Boss claim it to be the lowest cost option of any other form of water bombing. While the aircraft has only half the payload of a CL-415, it is just one tenth of the capital cost and one fifth of the operating cost. It says it costs just 64 cents (US) per gallon for water on a fire per hour. The aircraft has a 150kts ferry speed and a low drop speed of 105kts, making it more accurate. It can scoop 800 gallons in 15 seconds and has a 68-gallon foam capacity to help gel the water. With three plus hours between refuelling, it can drop 14,000 gallons per hour when the lake is near the fire. The drop is a computer-controlled Fire Retardant Dispersal System, and a two-seat version is available for either training or for a fire officer to control the movements from the back seat. The Fire Boss can take off on a lake in 2,200ft, and from land, there is a retractable landing gear in the floats, in 1,970ft and can climb when fully loaded at 892ft per minute. When the scoops are deployed, at landing speed, a water transfer tube moves the scooped water up through the float pylon and into the fuselage holding tank. In 2018, it was a very hot summer in Sweden and there were large fires – this is not a country used to such events. The government in Portugal loaned two Fire Boss aircraft, which worked as a pair. Lake Nora was 5.5 miles from the fire with a 4.5-minute circuit time. The aircraft performed 13 drops per hour for three hours.

First flown in February 1979, the Pacific Aerospace Corporation Cresco is built in Hamilton, New Zealand. It is a turboprop development of the piston-powered Fletcher FU-24, which dated back to 1954. Early production had a 600shp Lycoming LTP-700 turboprop and, for aircraft produced from 1992, a 750shp P&W Canada PT-6-34AG. The type is mostly used for crop dressing, but a water bomber version can be adapted with just small alterations from the normal use. In this role, it can drop its entire load of 238 gallons in one second or, in an hour, 6,350 gallons. One advantage of the type is its ability to operate from unpaved air strips.

Another crop duster that can operate as a water bomber is the PZL M.18A Dromader. The design work for this began in the mid-1970s by Polish company PZL-Mielec, and it first flew as a crop duster in August 1976 and as a water bomber two years later. Unlike the two previous types, the M.18A is powered by a 1,000hp ASz-621R nine-cylinder air-cooled radial piston engine. The hopper tank holds 450 gallons of water, plus 16 gallons of foaming agent, and is filled from a connector pipe under the fuselage. It can drop its entire load in one to two seconds or, if fitted for spraying, up to 17 seconds. Unlike the computer-controlled systems on some types, the drop is a mechanical operation with a large red handle in the cockpit, which opens the tank when pulled. The Dromader has been sold in more than 24 nations worldwide.

Above: Air Tractor AT-802 Fire Boss N6159F c/n 802A-0029 Tanker 85 is operated by Conair and is at Abbotsford in August 2005.

Left: AT-802 Fire Boss C-FLSI c/n 802A-0173 Tanker 82 is owned by Conair and is at their Abbotsford base in September 2008. It is in their house livery.

AT-802F CC-CNX c/n 802-0104 is operated by Faasa Aviación of Spain and carries the name Arauco, a Chilean wood company. It is at Tobalaba, Chile, in October 2003. This is the fixed undercarriage version of the AT-802F.

PZL M.18A Dromader EC-FAT c/n 1Z-022-03 is operated by the government of the Balearic Islands and is at Palma-Son Bonet, Spain, in September 2000.

Pacific Aerospace Cresco 08-600 ZK-LTW c/n 019 is operated by Aerowork, based at Wanganui. It is pictured flying and then dropping a load at Masterton Hood, New Zealand, in January 2013.

Chapter 9
Helicopters

Helicopters are becoming more and more important in the world of firefighting. There are two different types of role in which they are used. One is the specially tanked machine with dedicated systems and fixed roles on stations to await the call to arms. The other is the under slung bucket, which almost any helicopter in the world can carry, and is used when local services, be they private, government or air force, are called to a local area fire.

Of the first category, the most common is the large Sikorsky. It first flew in May 1962 as the CH-54 Tarhe and was designed for the US Army as a heavy lifter, carrying external loads or a specially designed pod. It was certified by the FAA in August 1969 for civil operations and was mostly used in the logging industry. The Erickson company based in Central Point, Oregon, was one of the users that saw a completely new role for the type, and, in February 1992, they took over the type certificate and manufacturing from Sikorsky. They remanufactured ex-army CH-54Bs and renamed them S-64F Helitankers. The engines were two 4,800shp P&W JTFD-12A turboshafts. That year also saw the fitting of a removable 2,650-gallon tank, plus capacity for 70 gallons of foam injection.

They have sold four aircraft to the forest service in Italy and also to the South Korean government. As well as this, they will contract their own aircraft and crews on a worldwide basis. They name each machine, and one S-64F was named *Elvis* and became quite a star in Australia, as it fought many bush fires there one year.

They can refill its tanks in any one of three ways: (1) from a normal land base to use either retardant or water; (2) a ram scoop hydrofoil attachment where the helicopter dips this into a lake and travels along the water filling the tank in under 40 seconds; (3) using a hover snorkel, where a large hose carried below the fuselage is dropped and hovers above the water source to suck up the water. It can fill its tanks in 45 seconds from water that can be a shallow as 18in. More than one swimming pool has been used to fill the tanks. The S-64F can drop 2,500 gallons every six minutes or 25,000 in an hour and, during an eight-hour day, can dump 200,000 gallons on a fire.

In 1997, a water cannon was developed specifically for the S-64F and was approved by the FAA the following year. This can be used for horizontal firefighting and can deliver 300 gallons per minute with a reach of 160ft. The flight crew of two have eight levels of selection for their drops. Following a fire, the tank can be used for hydroseeding, to restart forestation and prevent erosion. In a constant update of the design, 2007 saw upgrades to a glass cockpit.

From the former Soviet Union, the Kamov Design Bureau (OKB) has produced a line of helicopters with co-axial rotors, thus negating the need for a tail rotor. The Ka-27 is used by the Russian Navy and other air arms for anti-submarine warfare. The civil variant, the Ka-32, takes on many roles, one of which is firefighting. It can be fitted with an under-fuselage tank for either water or retardant. As well as this, it can use the bucket method on a line below the airframe; with this method, it can uplift up to 30 cycles an hour from a nearby water source.

The tank designed for the type is the Simplex Fire Attack Tank 328, which holds 785 gallons. It is made by Dent Aerospace of Portland, Oregon, and the helicopter is operated in more than 30 nations. The engines are a pair of 2,200shp Klimov-Isotov TV-3-117VMA turboshafts. The tank consists of a belly-mounted carbon fibreglass unit. It is cockpit controlled for the drop pattern and is quick to either install or remove. The dedicated fire version, the Ka-32A-11BC, can hover and refill with a hose fitted under the fuselage; it has a foam capacity of 40 gallons and a water cannon for horizontal fire suppression whilst in the hover mode. This, of course, could be used for tackling a blaze in a very tall building where the upper floors are on fire.

First flown in September 1961, the Boeing-Vertol CH-47 Chinook still serves with the US Army, as well as many other air arms around the world, as a heavy lift transport helicopter. In 60 years of operations, it has been upgraded over the years, and whilst the shape has remained the same, the interior, flight deck, performance and engines have been improved beyond recognition. As older airframes have reached the civil market and been refurbished, they have joined the ranks of water bombers in two different ways.

Based in Howell, Michigan, CHI Aviation's Chinooks use the long line bucket method for firefighting. The bucket system they use is the Powerfill Bambi Bucket. This has two methods of filling. The first is to lower it into a water supply, this can be as shallow as 18in, and then pumps in the bucket suck up the water. A combination of pumps can fill the bucket from 900 to 1,800 gallons per minute. Using the bucket manufacturer's own Torrentula Valve Technology, the pilot of the machine has the ability to perform unlimited drops at variable flow rates and split drops. The second method is to simply dip the whole bucket under the water and, when full, lift it out and proceed to the fire.

The Canadian company Coulson Aviation have a completely different system for their four CH-47D model of the Chinook. They have a roll-in-roll-out 3,000-gallon tank, which can be refilled on the ground at any water bomber base with either water or retardant at 500 gallons per minute, but the more usual method is to use the retractable snorkel system, the only one of its type. When this is lowered into the water supply, it takes just one minute to fill the tank. They claim it is the largest helitanker in service. When fitted with Coulson's own RADS-L tank, the Chinook has a 200in drop area in the floor to enable the maximum weight of water to hit the fire. This tank has a total of 16 different flow rates for dropping its load. Coulson started operations in 2019 with the Chinook, powered by a pair of 4,867shp Lycoming T-55 turboshafts, and they have brought the helicopter up to a new level with the latest technology, including the TCAS collision avoidance system and equipping and training the crews with Night Vision Goggles (NVG), so that night operations can be performed, and fire can be fought 24 hours a day seven days a week.

As mentioned in the beginning of this section, almost any helicopter can fight fires using an under slung bucket. The one that is in most common use is the Bambi Bucket made by SEI Industries of Delta, British Colombia. It was invented by Don Arney in 1978 and was a collapsible bucket with a pilot controlled valve for the release. He started the company and began production in 1982, and, today, they are sold worldwide. They are filled by either dipping into a lake or on the ground from a fire engine or hydrant. There are three models available. The basic one ranges in capacity from 72 to 2,590 gallons with 20 sizes to choose from, and they release the water in a single drop. The Bambi Max is able to split the load into multi-drops and has an emergency rapid shedding capability. The size range is from 180 to 2,590 gallons. The latest version is the Bambi Torrentula. This was introduced in 1997 and has bottom filling technology, the same as a snorkel, with fill rates of 1,700 gallons per minute. The size range is from 1,060 to 2,590 gallons.

Above: Bell UH-1H Iroquois N987SF c/n 8833 403 of the Nevada Department of Forestry is pictured at Minden in September 2010.

Right: Bell UH-1F N484DF c/n 7081 301 of the California Department of Forestry is pictured at Hemet Valley in September 1988.

Bell UH-1B N483DF c/n 7079 504 of the CDF is at Stockton in October 1984.

Bell UH-1H EC-GIV c/n 12481 is operated by the government of the Balearic Islands. It is pictured at Palma-Son Bonet in September 2000. Note the Bambi Bucket ready to be lifted and filled.

Bell UH-1H N409DF c/n 12375 of Cal Fire is undergoing maintenance at McClelland in May 2019.

Eurocopter AS550C3 Fennec E-384 c/n 7693 is operated by unit GAE-43 of Ejército Ecuatoriano (Ecuadorian Army) at Portoviejo Barracks, Ecuador, in October 2014. Note the Bambi Bucket in the foreground; it is an example of how almost any helicopter can fight fires.

Above, right and below right: PZL-Swidnik W-3A 0717 of the Czech Air Force is pictured arriving with a Bambi Bucket, then having it filled by fireman with a hose and later dropping its load. Pictured at Hradec Kralove, Czech Republic, in September 2010.

AgustaWestland AW119Ke Koala OH-HVL c/n 14733 is operated by the Rajavartiolaitos (Finnish Frontier Guards) and is pictured first flying with a Bambi Bucket and then dropping water at Tikkakoski, Finland, in June 2018.

Kamov Ka-32A11BC UP-K3201 c/n 523324069832 is operated by Kazakhstan's Ministry of Emergency Situations and is pictured at Astana (now known as Nur-Sultan), Kazakhstan, in June 2016.

A close-up of the Simplex Fire Attack tank on the Kamov Ka-32.

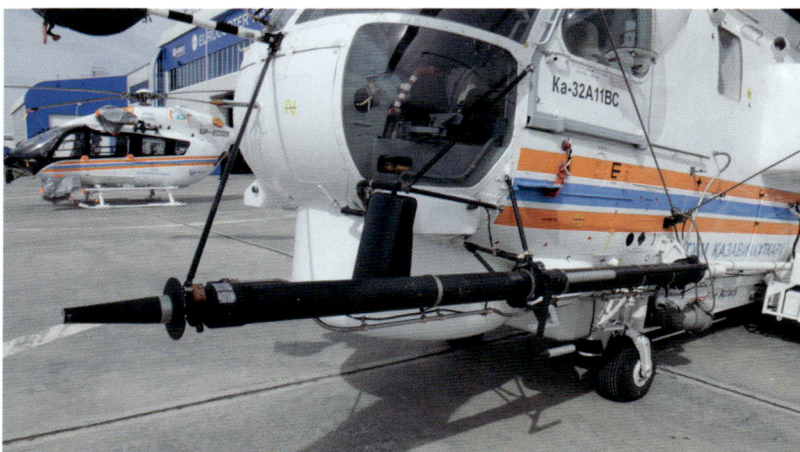

A close-up of the water cannon on the Kamov Ka-32, designed for horizontal firefighting.

Boeing CH-47D Chinook N950CH c/n M3459, operated by CHI Aviation, is pictured at McClellan in May 2019.

Sikorsky S-64B Skycrane N6962R c/n 64-058 Tanker 747 of Erickson Air Crane at Fox Field in May 2019.

S-64F Skycrane N179AC c/n 64-091 Tanker 739 of Erickson Air Crane is pictured flying at Oshkosh in July 2009.

S-64F N179AC dropping water at Oshkosh in July 2009. This aircraft is named *Elvis*.

S-64 Skycrane N6979R c/n 64-079 Tanker 707 of Evergreen Aviation is at Chico in October 2001. It was later sold to Helicopter Transport Services for the same role.

S-64/CH-54 Skycrane N9125M c/n 64-057 of Siller Helicopters is at Porterville in May 2019. The company is based at Yuba City, California. Note that the number on the tank is the last three characters of the registration.

Chapter 10
The Support Aircraft

Water bomber aircraft do not usually operate alone, they have aircraft to help them in their difficult task. This can take two forms; one is to act as a lead for the attack aircraft to follow and the second is for the support aircraft to circle above the fire area and direct the drop aircraft to the location needed for the water or retardant. The support types are many and varied but will usually be twin-engined for safety. Three types will be discussed.

The Cessna 336 Skymaster was first flown in February 1961, and from this came the model 337 with a retractable undercarriage and an up-rated 210hp Continental 10-360-C piston engine. It was a twin-boom aircraft, with one engine on the front and a second as a 'pusher' at the rear of the cabin. It was designed for the private flyer. In December 1966, it was ordered in volume, more than 500, by the US Air Force for Forward Air Control duties as the military model 0-2A. The main external difference was the clear vision panels in the cabin doors, which gave the pilot a better view of the area he was patrolling, as it was, of course, the era of the Vietnam War. Upon retirement from the USAF, many were used by other government or state agencies as the support aircraft for water bombers, and on many a base, a Cessna 0-2A would be parked next to the air attack aircraft, ready to go off to deal with a fire.

Since the Martin Mars was a pure flying boat, the support aircraft or 'bird dog' aircraft was an amphibian, a Grumman G-21A Goose. The type dated back to a first flight in May 1937 and was powered by a pair of 450hp P&W R-985 Wasp Junior radial piston engines. When it was called to action, it would taxi down a ramp from its base into Sproat Lake, retract the undercarriage and take off on the water ahead of the Mars. It would then race to the fire to advise the giant flying boat that was following what sort of fire it was and the best path to attack it from.

The current support/bird dog for Cal Fire is the North American Rockwell OV-10A Bronco. Built in Columbus, Ohio, it first flew in July 1965 and its role was in a counter-insurgency (COIN) operation as a light attack aircraft. Its first customer was the US Marine Corps and then the US Air Force. It has also been sold to a number of other air arms. In 1993, California acquired 15 for the role of water bomber support and the military equipment, guns and armour were removed. This made it a light and very hot ship to fly, and it was powered by 715shp Garrett T-76 turboprops. The aircraft has two tasks, the first of which is to take the air attack officer to the site of the fire. This person is a very experienced and well-trained fire officer who has the job of co-ordinating with the commander on the ground as to where to drop the retardant. When not doing that, it acts as a lead aircraft for the tanker to follow for its drop. There is a crew of two, a pilot and a chief officer or fire captain.

With the climate changing and more extremes of weather both hot and cold taking place, water bombers will be on the front line to protect the forests of the world and stop them from burning. As this is written, two fires in the western US have destroyed over one million acres. Water and retardant from the sky will be with us for many years to come.

Cessna 0-2A N467DF c/n 337-0290 A41 of the CDF is at Porterville in October 1979. Note that, on the 0-2 variant, the doors have clear panels for extra visibility for the pilot.

Above and right: Grumman G-21A Goose C-FVFU c/n B-101 of Forest Industries Flying Tankers at Sproat Lake, Vancouver Island, is pictured in September 1984. It was sold to a company in Croatia in 2001 but is now back in Canada and reregistered as C-FMXW.

North American T-28B Trojan N218SF c/n 200-351 is operated by the Nevada Department of Forestry whilst on loan from the Alaska Department of Forestry. It is pictured at Douglas County Airport in September 1988.

Ted Smith Aerostar 600A C-GSXX c/n 60-0430-146 is operated by Conair and pictured at Abbotsford in May 2000.

Bell 209 AH-1G Huey Cobra N109Z c/n 20854 of the USFS is at Fox Field in October 2006. It is still current with them.

Bell AH-1F N347WN c/n 22167 No 7, operated by the Washington State Department of Natural Resources. It is at Olympia, Washington, in June 2009. The registration was cancelled in April 2011, and it is now in a museum in Amarillo, Texas.

Beech B200GT Super King Air N741JR c/n BY-103 is operated by the USFS at Porterville in May 2019.

Beech A200CT Super King Air N463DF c/n BP-024 A504 of Cal Fire is at McClelland in May 2019.

Right: North American Rockwell OV-10A Bronco N415DF c/n 305-038 460 of Cal Fire is at its Ramona base in May 2019.

Below: A pair of OV-10 Broncos of Cal Fire await their flights to their summer bases. Pictured at McClelland in May 2019.

Bottom: A line of five OV-10 Broncos are pictured at McClelland in May 2006. At this time, they still carry the old CDF name rather than the current Cal Fire.

Casa 212-200 N117BH c/n 171 of Sheridan, Wyoming-based Bighorn Airways. It is pictured outside the Alaska Smokejumpers HQ at US Army base Fort Wainwright in May 2000. It is the largest aircraft in their mixed fleet of aircraft. The smokejumpers are a branch of the Alaska Fire Service and Bureau of Land Management. Their role is to parachute into remote areas to suppress wildfires. The aircraft can carry up to 12 smokejumpers, chainsaws, water pumps and supplies for three days.

Further reading from

As Europe's leading aviation publisher, we also produce a wide range of market-leading magazines.

Visit: shop.keypublishing.com for more details

KEY.AERO Your Aviation Destination - Visit www.Key.Aero today